Browns Index to Photocomposition Typography

BROWNS INDEX

TO PHOTOCOMPOSITION TYPOGRAPHY

A compendium of terminologies, procedures
and constraints for the guidance of
designers, editors and publishers

written and compiled by BRUCE BROWN MA (RCA) FRSA

edited by S W GREENWOOD

GREENWOOD
PUBLI

Bruce Brown was born in Glasgow, Scotland. He studied Graphic Design in Liverpool and Canterbury and gained his Masters Degree at the Royal College of Art in London. He is at present the art director of *Crafts Magazine*, the Head of Graphic Design at Norwich School of Art and the external assessor to the degree course in graphics at Maidstone College of Art. In the past Mr Brown has gained many awards for his work, undertaking professional commissions for a wide variety of clients as well as teaching responsibilities at the Royal College of Art and Middlesex Polytechnic. He has published articles on design in many professional journals including *Design*, *Penrose Annual*, *Information Design Journal*, *Printing World*, also two papers published at the Royal College of Art and the text of a lecture delivered at the Centre Georges Pompidou, Paris. He lives in Norwich with his wife and two cats.

Stanley Greenwood in his early career studied typography at London's Central School of Art & Design, while apprenticed as display compositor to nearby letterpress printer the John Roberts Press. He entered publishing in 1946 following RAF wartime service during which he was awarded the DFC. Publishing began with magazines and books on photography and cinematography, and he entered the graphic arts publishing scene on joining Northwood Publications – part of the Thomson Organisation – in 1966. As a Publisher within Northwood he was responsible for building up a graphic arts group of publications which included *Printing Today*, *Newspaper Report*, *Print Buyer*, *Packaging Today*, *Paper Facts & Figures* – and from 1973 *The Penrose Annual*. On the sale of the group in 1981 he accepted an early retirement from Northwood to publish independently from the quiet of his home in Somerset.

This book, designed by
Bruce Brown, has been typeset
and printed by
Jolly & Barber Ltd, Rugby.

The typesetting has been
generated on a Monotype 1000
system using 96 relative units to
the em.

With the exception of Part II, set
in 10pt Gill Sans, this book has
otherwise been set throughout in
Rockwell using mainly 9 on 10 pt
light and bold. Letterspacing has
been specified at 0 units and
wordspacing at 20 units.

First edition 1983
Published by Greenwood
Publishing
The Tallet, Church Street,
Minehead, Somerset, England

ISBN 0 946824 00 2

Acknowledgments. This *Index* has taken a great deal of time and effort to compile and prepare. Herbert Spencer and Romek Marber first saw the potential in the idea and directed me, independently, to Stanley Greenwood who, with Clive Goodacre, took the idea on board. Without my publisher's faith, patience and efforts this project would have surely collapsed. Publisher and author are indebted to all those manufacturers, suppliers and designers who have provided information and for their permission to publish the same.

Contents

Author's Preface

Developments in photocomposition technology accrue at such an exhausting pace that even the most experienced designers and make-up personnel are bewildered by the ever-changing profusion of terminologies, procedures and constraints.

Such circumstances can only serve to throw a strait-jacket around the freewill and judgment of all who are required to design for type. In response to this challenge the contents and the form of this index to photocomposition typography have been specifically devised to provide easily accessible facts, figures and formulae.

This is not a book to read, or to be used exclusively as a source of reference. This is a practical working handbook which is intended to be *used* at the drawing board, make-up desk – or even at the kitchen table. To this end the form of the work has been devised to contain the greatest amount of information within the least amount of space, hopefully making the contents both invaluable and easily portable.

My objective when devising the *Index* was no grander than to provide an efficient working tool through which designers with type may have the opportunity to exercise greater control and personal judgment over the typographic problems they are required to tackle.

11

Introduction

Browns Index was conceived as a working tool
for what is now the major form of typesetting to the
design professions and printing industries. It has been
devised therefore to carry valuable and exhaustive
information within an accessible and easily portable
format. Although it does contain extensive information
on photocomposition systems, typefaces as affected by
photocomposition and copyfitting procedures, the
Index is *not* simply a textbook, specimen book or
instruction course to the discipline. More than this, the
concept behind its compilation has been twofold;

1 to provide a specific source of easily retrievable
information on the procedures, terminologies and
constraints of photocomposition typography. This
source of information will prove invaluable to both
students and professionals alike.

2 To provide a method of enhancing the means by
which such information may be controlled and
manipulated by the designer to provide a wider range
of typographic solutions. This is particularly so where
difficult copyfitting calculations need to be made.

Following this concept Parts I, II, III and IV provide the
information: Part I an explanation of terminologies,

illustrated and as comprehensive as it has been possible to make it; Part II demonstrates the variable effects that may be achieved through the manipulation of character and interline spacing; Part III lists the mechanical constraints of photocomposition systems important to the user, and Part IV the extensive range of photocomposition typefaces currently available.

Copyfitting is confined to Parts V and VI, the former listing typefactors for the major part of the typeface range and printed on a tinted stock to provide a distinctive marker for the copyfitting sections. The pocket calculator programs of Part VI are also clearly divided into sections for single line calculations, for bodytext and for running text in order to facilitate quick reference and use.

Inevitably, any publication of this kind will be hard pressed to keep abreast of such fast moving technological progress. This is of particular relevance in Part III, Machine Constraints. Here the reader is advised to initially use the tables as a basic guide and then to contact their typesetting house to ensure that all of the options listed are available or that significant modifications to the manufacturer's standard specification have not been made.

Care has been taken to make *Browns Index* not only comprehensive but also simple to use. With only a little practice the user will master even the most complex typographic problems.

How to use Browns Index

Part I. Photocomposition typography: terms and explanations. The alphabetical listing of descriptive terms has been compiled to provide both general background information and specific facts related to the design of type for photocomposition systems. Each entry has been cross-referenced as shown in the following example:

(*character*/*cross stroke*/SEE descender)

In this case the reference is concerned with a sequential chain of entries all referring to the nomenclature for parts of typographic characters. *Character* is the first entry at which the chain of descriptive terms begins. *Cross stroke* is the entry prior to the one accessed by the user, and descender comes immediately afterwards in the chain.

By using this method, the user will be able to move backwards and forwards through a sequence of linked descriptions until a satisfactory explanation has been achieved. Words italicised within each explanation also provide a secondary source of reference.

Terminologies and abbreviations used throughout *Browns Index* have been included in Part I, as have additional computing instructions for converting linear dimensions. (SEE conversion tables)

Part II. Spacing type for photocomposition: examples of alternative specifications. Because modern photocomposition systems can control the spacing of type with greater flexibility and in minute detail, it is important for the designer to appreciate the effects on both the readability and appearance of type caused by modifications to intercharacter and interlinear spacing. It is also important to remember that each photocomposition system may vary the magnitude of the smallest increment by which modifications can be made. It is hoped that these selective examples of variable spacing will provide the basic guidance on which further design decisions may be made.

Part III. Photocomposition systems: important machine constraints. A table of machine constraints is provided for the majority of photocomposition systems in current use. Each table is divided into eight separate numbered divisions, grouping the constraints important to typographic and copyfitting problems:

1 Typesizes
2 Letter and interline spacing
3 Mixing typefaces and sizes
4 Output material
5 Hyphenation and tabbing
6 Rules
7 Fount make-up
8 Fount storage and retrieval

Each of the technical descriptions used in this section are explained in Terminology, Part I, to which the user should refer for clarification where necessary. The user will also find division 2 of each table 'Letter and interline spacing' most useful when used in conjunction with the copyfitting typefactors and programs of Parts V and VI. For example the user may wish to copyfit using a modified typefactor for *minus letterspacing*, and in this case prior knowledge of the number of relative units to the em is essential. Alternatively, use of the copyfitting programs may suggest that *interline spacing* of 2.5pt was required, and this would be impracticable for the user without knowledge of the chosen systems' ability to produce horizontal spacing in half-point increments. Other information contained in the tables will give the user general guidance when specifying typesetting on a specific photocomposition system.

Part IV. Photocomposition typefaces: a guide to typestyles and families. The tables here list the extensive range of photocomposition typefaces in current use. The name of each typeface (set in bold) is given in alphabetical order, with solid 'bullets' appearing under an abbreviation of each manufacturer's name. The typeface names set in light face following within the same 'family box' are the alternatives used by other manufacturers for their own particular version of the same typeface. Manufacturers using the alternative names are indicated in the tables by an outline 'bullet'. In this format the tables provide an invaluable source of cross-reference to the variety of names by which different systems' manufacturers will refer to a single typeface. For example, **Melior** is alternatively referred to as Ballardvale, Hanover, Mallard, ME, Medallion and Uranus. Reference to the lists will therefore be of assistance to the user in moving a typographic specification from one photocomposition system to another.

Part V. Copyfitting for photocomposition: typefactors for variable fount widths. Because the variable widths of all characters making up a complete alphabet have no constancy from one typeface design to another, or from one photocomposition system to another, some means of quantifying this relative design width of typefaces and setting systems is required in order to make reliable typographic calculations.

In *Browns Index* a unique 'typefactor' has been introduced for use with the copyfitting programs. Each typefactor is separately calculated to express the relative width of a typeface and hence the number of characters to a specified measure. With the following instructions and a pocket calculator the user will be able to convert any typefactor into the average number of upper/lower case characters to a measure;

AC	measure in picas
÷	typesize in points
×	typefactor
=	calculator display shows the number of upper and lower case characters

For the more complex computations required with everyday copyfitting the typefactor must be used in conjunction with the copyfitting programs, Part VI.

It should be noted that the typefactors calculated for *Browns Index* relate to type set with normal letter and word spacing. Should the inter-character spacing be varied, either by the addition or subtraction of relative units, then the typefactor must also be modified accordingly. This may be achieved by reference to the step-by-step instructions for computing a modified typefactor, page 226.

It may also be that a chosen typeface is not listed in the

typefactors. However, if a sample of the set text or of the lower case alphabet is available to the user, then the typefactor can be computed by referring to the typefactor calculating instructions on page 227. Here it must be added that the most reliable means of copyfitting may be achieved by obtaining an actual sample of the setting to be used, and from this to calculate a typefactor using the instructions on page 227. In this case the higher the character count, then the greater the accuracy.

Part VI. Copyfitting for photocomposition: programs for a pocket calculator. The copyfitting programs in *Browns Index* are pre-calculated step-by-step instructions for use with a pocket calculator. They have been specifically formulated to assist the user in computing the missing element in an often complex typographic specification.

The programs are intended for use with most simple pocket calculators. The only special function keys required are a single memory store (store and recall) and, though not used frequently, a square root facility. These functions may be identified in a variety of ways on different calculators, but the symbols used for them in the copyfitting programs are as follows:

M+   add information shown on the calculator display to that in the memory and store for use at a later stage in the computation

MR   recall information which has been stored in the memory at an earlier stage of the computation

M−   subtract information shown on the calculator display from that stored in the memory

√   square root function

AC switch the calculator on in preparation for computing and erase all information on the display and that stored in the memory

C erase information on the calculator display without disturbing the memory

Should any of the above symbols differ from those of the user's calculator then amendments to the copyfitting programs may be made where appropriate and necessary. To check the working order of the calculator and its function keys a hypothetical example has been included with each program under the heading 'test'. At the end of this section a record sheet has been included (pages 318–319) on which the user may record alternative calculations to a single problem.

Should any of the measuring systems used in these programs need to be converted into any other, then instructions for so doing will be found under *conversion tables* in Part I.

It must be said of the copyfitting programs that while the use of a pocket calculator makes increasingly complex typographic computations more effective and less repetitive, it does *not* ensure that results are always one hundred per cent accurate. No copyfitting system can make this claim, and whilst the system used here is believed to be the most reliable, rapid and comprehensive of those currently available, less reliable results may be likely where, for example, a large typesize is set to an exceptionally short measure, where a typesetting house has modified the unit spacing without the knowledge of the user, or where the calculation is used for a language other than English on which the typefactors are based.

Part I Terminology

aa   abbreviation for *authors alteration*

accents   (*SEE* DIACRITICAL MARKS)

acute é   (DIACRITICAL MARKS/*SEE* BAR 1)

adaptable fractions   large or full sized diagonal
fractions made up from three separate
characters, eg 3/4; also known as *built fraction*
(FRACTIONS/*SEE* COMBINATION FRACTION)

agate line   system of measurement used in
newspaper design;
14 agates = 1 inch
(MEASURING SYSTEMS/IMPERIAL SYSTEM/*SEE* UNIT SYSTEM)

algol   (*SEE* LANGUAGE)

algorithm   a logic based method of problem solving
(*SEE* FLOWCHART)

aliassing   used to describe the inaccuracies caused
by *digitising* subtle geometric shapes onto a
fixed rectangular grid

alphanumeric   a set of alphabetic characters and
numerals (CLASSIFICATION OF TYPE/*SEE* ROMAN NUMERALS)

ABCDEFGHIJKLMNOPQRS TUVWXYZabcdefghijklmno pqrstuvwxyz1234567890

ampersand   symbol for 'and' derived from the
Latin et (FOUNT/PI CHARACTERS/*SEE* COMMERCIAL @)

analog computer   works by representing numbers
as a physical quantity such as the rotation of shafts,
gear wheels or the intensity of an electrical charge;
a traditional clock is an analog device;
these types of computers are never used in
photocomposition systems as they do not have
the storage or logic capacity of digital machines
(*SEE* DIGITAL COMPUTER)

antiqua   typefaces having *old face* letterforms

apex   upper points of the junctions of the *stems* of
characters such as A, M, W, which meet at less
than 90° (CHARACTER/DESCENDER/*SEE* CROSSED STEM)

arabic numerals   standard means of marking
numbers by the use of symbols originating from
India and Arabia and adopted by the Spanish
around 1000 AD
(CLASSIFICATION OF TYPE/ROMAN NUMERALS/*SEE* LATIN ALPHABET)

1234567890

arm   the projecting, unclosed, or short oblique
strokes in characters such as E, L, C, S
(CHARACTER/TAIL/*SEE* SPINE)

ascender   the parts of some *lower case* characters
such as b, d, h, which rise above the *x-height* or
mean line (CHARACTER/CROSS STROKE/*SEE* DESCENDER)

ascender line   an imaginary line running along the
tops of *ascenders*
(*MEASURING TYPE*/*BASELINE*/*SEE* CAPITAL LINE)

bcdefg

asterisk *   first order reference mark
(*FOUNT*/*REFERENCE MARKS*/*SEE* DAGGER)

authors alterations (aa)   marked on proofs to signify
corrections which are the authors responsibility
(US equivalent is *pe* or printers error)
(*PROOF CORRECTION MARKS*/*PRINTERS ERROR*/*SEE* GALLEY PROOF)

authors correction   same as *authors alteration*

authors proof   initial proof supplied to the
client/author on which the printer's reader has
marked corrections and queries
(*PROOF CORRECTION MARKS*/*GALLEY PROOF*/*SEE* MASTER PROOF)

automatic typeface mix   (*SEE* TYPEFACE MIX WITHIN A LINE)

B

backslant   those typefaces inclined to the left
(*CLASSIFICATION OF TYPE*/*ITALIC*/*SEE* MONOLINE)

bar 1) ∅ (DIACRITICAL MARK/ACUTE/*SEE* BOLL)
2) a closed horizontal stroke in characters
(CHARACTER/CROSSED STEM/*SEE* TAIL)

HAe

barrel printer a class of line printer in which all of
the characters are placed around the surface of a
cylinder which rotates at high speed, the
required character being selected as it comes
opposite a print hammer
(HARDWARE/MATRIX PRINTER/*SEE* CHAIN PRINTER)

baseline an imaginary line running along the base of
most *lower case* letters
(MEASURING TYPE/*SEE* ASCENDER LINE)

abcde

baseline alignment the normal method used by
typesetting systems for aligning type
(*SEE* TOP ALIGNMENT)

BASE ALIGNING

BASIC (*SEE* LANGUAGE)

bastard size   any typographic measurement which
does not conform to an adopted, standard
system, of calculation (*SEE* MEASURING SYSTEMS)

beak   one-sided *serif* on the *arms* of characters such
as E, F, C, G, T, Z (CHARACTER/SERIF/*SEE* FOOT)

bi-directional line printer   a line printer which can
operate both from left-to-right and from right-to-
left , thereby doubling the speed at which *hard
copy* may be produced
(HARDWARE/LINE PRINTER/*SEE* MATRIX PRINTER)

binary code   a coding system which can convert any
numeric values into a sequence of yes/no
questions and answers for storage and retrieval
in a *computer*

binary digit   a digit in *binary notation* either, 1 or 0,
and generally abbreviated as *bit*

binary notation   a positional notation system for
representing numbers and having a *radix* of two;
numbers are represented by the two digits 0 and
1 and each displacement of one digit position to
the left means that the digit is multiplied by a
factor of 2;
often the coding system employed in computer
programs because of its basic yes/no alternatives;

example:

$$\begin{array}{|c|c|c|c|c|} 16 & 8 & 4 & 2 & 1 \\ 0 & 0 & 0 & 1 & 0 \end{array} = 2$$

$$\begin{array}{|c|c|c|c|c|c|} 32 & 16 & 8 & 4 & 2 & 1 \\ 1 & 0 & 0 & 1 & 0 & 1 \end{array} = 37$$

therefore:

0000 = 0	0100 = 4	1000 = 8
0001 = 1	0101 = 5	1001 = 9
0010 = 2	0110 = 6	1010 = 10
0011 = 3	0111 = 7	and so on

(NUMBER SYSTEMS/DECIMAL NOTATION/*SEE* POSITIONAL REPRESENTATION)

bit   contraction for *binary digit*;
a set of binary digits are called a *byte*

black face   synonymous for *bold face*
(*SEE* TYPEFACE WEIGHT)

black letter   a group of typefaces evolved from the
broad-nib penstyle of gothic lettering used by
scribes in Northern Europe. Also known as *Old
English*
(CLASSIFICATION OF TYPE/SCRIPT/*SEE* COPPERPLATE SCRIPT)

𝕬𝕭𝕮𝕯𝕰𝕱𝕲𝕳𝕴𝕵𝕶𝕷𝕸𝕹𝕺𝕻
𝕼𝕽𝕾𝕿𝖀𝖁𝖂𝖃𝖄𝖅abcdefghijkl
mnopqrstuvwxyz 1234567890

blind keyboard   in photocomposition a tape-
producing keyboard which does not display to
the operator the copy being keyboarded
(HARDWARE/NON-COUNTING KEYBOARD/*SEE* DIRECT KEYBOARD)

block diagram   (*SEE* FLOWCHART)

blue-line/blueprints/blues   (*SEE* OZALID PROOF)

bodytext   an area, or column of type, usually in the
size range of 5–14pt (LAYOUT/RUN-AROUND/*SEE* MEASURE)

bold   contraction for *bold face* (*SEE* TYPEFACE WEIGHT)

bold face   the relative blackness of a typeface where
strokes have been thickened (*SEE* TYPEFACE WEIGHT)

Helioprint
Helioprint
Helioprint

boll å (DIACRITICAL MARKS/BAR/*SEE* CEDILLA)

bowl the oval or circular forms of characters, either
complete as in O, Q or partial as in P, p
(CHARACTER/POTHOOK/*SEE* EAR)

BCDG
OPQR

box rules a term used in the tables of photocomposition systems, Part III of this book, to
identify whether or not different photocomposition systems can automatically set
vertical/horizontal rules within text areas

brace come in a number of sizes and used to join two
or more lines of type eg

Gill Sans
{ light
medium
bold
condensed

(FOUNT/SOLIDUS/*SEE* ELLIPSES)

brackets () or [ ] also known as parentheses and
used to enclose matter not essential to the
meaning of a sentence, asides by the author or
references within the text (FOUNT/EM RULE/*SEE* SOLIDUS)

bracketed serifs   serifs joined to the stem of the character by a continuous curve *(SEE* LATIN/SERIF*)*

breve ŏ   curved line over a vowel indicating that it is short *(*DIACRITICAL MARKS/UMLAUTT */SEE* MACRON*)*

bromide   usual form of photographic material and having a paper base *(SEE* OUTPUT MATERIAL*)*

brownprint   *(SEE* OZALID PROOF*)*

brush script   a group of typefaces having the appearance of free-hand drawing with a brush, eg Ashley Script
*(*CLASSIFICATION OF TYPE/COPPERPLATE SCRIPT */SEE* IONIC*)*

ABCDEFGHIJKLMNOPQRSTUV
WXYZabcdefghijklmnopqrstuv
wxyz1234567890
ABCDEF

BS   prefix for British Standards Institution *(SEE* LINEALE*)*

built fraction   *(SEE* ADAPTABLE FRACTION*)*

bullet ●   typographic mark in the form of a large dot and commonly used to give emphasis *(SEE* FOUNT*)*

byte   in computer programming a set of *bits* making up one alphabetic, numerical or special character

calligraphy the art of beautiful handwriting
(*SEE* DOWNSTROKE)

CALLIGR

cardinal numbers the regular sequence of numbers one, two, three etc – as opposed to *ordinal numbers*, first, second, third etc

carry forward American term for *take over*

case fraction small fractions designed as a single unit, eg $^3/_4$ and also known as solid fractions. They may also be available as horizontal fractions ($\frac{3}{4}$)
(FRACTIONS/COMBINATION FRACTIONS/*SEE* PIECE FRACTION)

cassette (*SEE* MAGNETIC TAPE CASSETTE)

cast off (*SEE* CHARACTER COUNT)

cap height the height of capital letters (*SEE* CAPITAL LINE)

capital line when no lower case characters with ascenders appear, an imaginary line running along the tops of capital letters. Capital height is measured from baseline to capital line
(MEASURING TYPE/ASCENDER LINE/*SEE* MEANLINE)

ABCD

caps contraction for capitals (*SEE* UPPER CASE)

cathode ray tube (crt)   an electronic tube of which
the surface is coated with *phosphor*;
a beam of electrons directed towards the front of
the tube energise the phosphor on contact to
produce a light image;
the electron beam sweeps the screen in lines
called *rasters* and thereby builds up an image on
the visual display unit

(HARDWARE /MARCHING DISPLAY UNIT /SEE SCROLLING FACILITY)

cedilla ç   (DIACRITICAL MARKS /BOLL /SEE CIRCUMFLEX)

centimetre (cm)   increment in the metric system of
measurement;
1 cm = 10 mm
100 cm = 1 m

(MEASURING SYSTEMS /MILLIMETRE /SEE IMPERIAL SYSTEM)

central processing unit (cpu)   (SEE COMPUTER)

centre   in *bodytext* where each line is to a different
measure – a layout whereby the column is left
ragged equally to both the left and to the right

(LAYOUT /RANGE /SEE COLUMN DEPTH)

Fine typography is the result of
nothing more than an attitude. Its appeal
comes from the typographic
understanding used in its planning;
the designer must always care.
In contemporary advertising, the perfect
integration of design elements may
demand typography that is unorthodox.
This could mean using tight
spacing, minus leading and different
sizes and weights.

centre alignment   the ability of some photocomposing machines to set individual letters midway between the *baseline* and *capital line* (*SEE* BASELINE ALIGNMENT)

CENTRE ALIGNING

chain printer   a class of high speed line printer in which the characters are carried past the paper by the links of a continuous chain
(BARREL PRINTER /*SEE* HARDWARE)

chancery italic   roman handwriting style of 15th century (CLASSIFICATION OF TYPE /GLYPHIC /*SEE* SCRIPT)

H *ic elegos? tm pune diem consum pserit ingens*
T *elephus? aut summi plena iam margine libri*
S *criptus, et in tergo nec dum finitus, Orestes?*
N *otu magis nulli domus est sua, quam mihi*

character   in any *typeface* prepared for mechanical reproduction a single typographic sign
1) (*SEE* CHARACTER STROKE) or 2) (FOUNT /*SEE* UPPER CASE)

character assembly   the assembly of *characters* by a photo unit, and in a form suitable for reproduction by a printing medium; character assembly is a general term and in photocomposition systems the two main categories are *character formation* and *character projection*
(HARDWARE /PHOTO UNIT /*SEE* CHARACTER PROJECTION)

character capacity   the total number of characters capable of being retrieved from a photo-composition system may be deduced by multiplying the number of *founts per master* by the number of characters per fount then by the number of *image masters* in the machine

character count   the process of calculating the
number of letters and spaces in a typewriter
manuscript;
because typewriters produce a consistent
number of characters to the inch (normally 10 or
12) this calculation is fairly simple

```
When working from typescript, a quick
and accurate character count can be
made by drawing a vertical line down
the right-hand side of the copy so as
to cut-off the 'ragged ends' of the
typed lines, leaving lines containing
an equal number of characters and
spaces. By multiplying the number of
characters and spaces in such a line
by the number of lines in the copy,
and adding on the extra spaces and
characters in the 'ragged ends' you
can find the total number of charac-
ters and spaces in the copy.
```

character exposure   in photocomposition, the ability
of a *character generator* to project the individual
characters held in an image master on to light
sensitive paper or film and through a glass or
fibre optical lens system;
In those systems based on the principle of
character projection the generator is a very
strong pulsed light source (eg the Linoterm HS
uses pulsed xenon) and each character exposure
is called a *flash*;
in some cases the image masters may be in the

form of a film drum with an internal light source;
in other photocomposition systems based on the
principle of *character formation* the generating
light source may be either a *cathode ray tube*
(crt) or a *laser* beam;

with a crt the generating electron beams not only
illuminate the selected phosphor particles but
also those surrounding the target area causing a
distortion to the original character image;

crt light sources track a vertically scanned,
digitized image;

where a laser beam is used as the generating
light source in *character formation*, its *coherent*
beam ensures that no such halation or distortion
to the original character image will occur;

laser beams track a horizontally scanned,
digitized image producing finer quality on
bracketed serifs

(HARDWARE/IMAGE CARRIER/*SEE* OUTPUT MATERIAL)

character fit   (*SEE* LETTERFIT)

character formation   in character assembly by
photocomposition systems this term may be
explained best with reference to the relaying of
an image from its source to the final resolution on
a television screen;

here the original character image must be
broken down into a series of units stored digitally
in the computer (the process is called *digitisation*)
and then transferred through space as a series of
unrecognisable electronic impulses to its final
point of *resolution*

(HARDWARE/CHARACTER PROJECTION/*SEE* IMAGE MASTER)

character generator   in photocomposition systems
the component that realises the characters from
their stored form in an image master

(*SEE* CHARACTER EXPOSURE)

character grid   (*SEE* IMAGE MASTER)

characters per pica (cpp)   a method used by some
  manufacturers to assist designers with
  copyfitting problems;
  each fount is given a number, equivalent to the
  number of characters that will make each pica
  (or 12pt) em and for a given typesize (*SEE* TYPEFACTOR)

characters per second (cps)   the speed at which a
  photo unit can perform character assembly;
  for further details see tables for photocomposition
  systems, Part III of this book
  (HARDWARE/OUTPUT RESOLUTION/*SEE* LPM)

characters per typeface   the number of characters in
  a typeface is not standard and, depending on
  foreign accents and other signs, may range from
  90–200

character projection   in character assembly by
  photocomposition systems this term may be
  explained best with reference to the projection of
  an image in a cinema;
  here a light source is projected through a small
  piece of film holding the original image and then
  through optical lenses enlarging and
  reproducing the image on to a screen
  (HARDWARE/CHARACTER ASSEMBLY/*SEE* CHARACTER FORMATION)

character space   (*SEE* LETTERSPACE)

character stroke   individual linear element of a
  typographic character (CHARACTER/*SEE* SHEAR)

cicero   a standard typographic unit in most European
  countries with one cicero being equal to 12 didot
  points (MEASURING SYSTEMS/PICA/*SEE* METRIC SYSTEM)

circumflex ô   derived from a mark signifying a
  contraction (DIACRITICAL MARKS/CEDILLA/*SEE* DIAERESIS)

classification of type   there are but a few, if any,
  comprehensive and generally accepted
  categories for the classification of type:

however, the following groupings may prove
useful

1) cultural differences (*SEE* ALPHANUMERIC)

2) historical development (*SEE* SERIFS (2))

3) typestyles derived from writing /cutting
instruments (*SEE* STYLUS)

4) general appearance, ie weight, etc (*SEE* ROMAN)

client proof   synonymous for *authors proof*

close up   instruction on *proof* to reduce space
between characters, words or lines of text
(*SEE* PROOF CORRECTION MARKS)

cm   abbreviation for *centimetre*

COBAL   (*SEE* LANGUAGE)

coherent   term applied to a beam of light where each
side of the beam is, and will remain, parallel to
the other;
a *laser* is a beam of coherent light;
all other light sources are non-coherent

colon :   used after a part of a sentence which is
complete in itself but when the sense of what
follows arises naturally from the former;
in such cases the first letter after the colon is
lower case;
also used to introduce a list, and expressions
of time;
a colon is usually placed outside quotation marks
unless it is part of the quoted matter
(FOUNT /COMMA /*SEE* SEMICOLON)

column depth   bodytext, in which the depth of the
area of type is specified in either pica ems or in
lines of type, ie 44 lines of 10/12pt
(LAYOUT /CENTRE /*SEE* RUNNING TEXT)

combination fraction   similar to *adaptable fraction*,
being made up from three separate characters
but using small numerals, eg $^3/_4$
(FRACTIONS /ADAPTABLE FRACTIONS /*SEE* CASE FRACTIONS)

comma , used to indicate small pauses between clauses within a sentence;
if used with a quotation mark, it always appears within the mark (FOUNT /FULL POINT /*SEE* COLON)

commercial @ special character meaning 'at'
(FOUNT /AMPERSAND /*SEE* COPYRIGHT MARK)

compatibility the ability of one photocomposition system to operate under commands from the computer program of a quite different composing system
(HARDWARE /INTELLIGENT TERMINAL /*SEE* VISUAL EDITING TERMINAL)

composition size all *typesizes* up to 14pt and used mainly for the setting of text
(CLASSIFICATION OF TYPE /SHADOW /*SEE* DISPLAY SIZE)

computer in computerised photocomposition the item of hardware which accepts data in a prescribed or coded form and then manipulates the data to automatically control a further machine or process such as the editing terminal or the photo unit
(HARDWARE /READ-WRITE HEAD /*SEE* STAND ALONE)

computerised composition synonymous with, but inadequate for *computerised photocomposition*; in this inaccurate sense the term would refer to any method of typesetting, eg hot metal, driven by a computer

computerised photocomposition in this method of typesetting the keyboard and photo unit of the photocomposition system are augmented by a third unit called either a computer or a central processing unit;
the function of this third unit is to remember instructions so that it may assist in the making of very detailed and rapid calculations
(PHOTOCOMPOSITION /*SEE* HARDWARE)

computer languages (*SEE* LANGUAGE)

computer program (*SEE* PROGRAM)

computer typesetting synonymous with but less
adequate for *computerised photocomposition*;
in this inaccurate sense the term could refer to
any method of typesetting (eg by hot metal or the
computer itself) driven by a computer.

condensed one of the many variants to the relative
width of a typeface (*SEE* TYPEFACE WIDTH)

conversion tables along with a pocket caculator the
factors shown below will enable the designer or
compositor to convert any linear dimension into
any other by using the following method:

example: how many millimetres are there in two
ciceros?

method:

2	×	*20.775*	÷	*4.586*	=	9.06
CICEROS		*CICERO FACTOR*		*MILLIMETRE FACTOR*		MILLIMETRES

therefore 2 ciceros equals 9.06 millimetres

conversion factors

MEASURING SYSTEMS	INCREMENTS	CONVERSION FACTORS
Anglo-American	point	1.618
	pica	19.416
Didot	point	1.724
	cicero	20.689
Agate	agate	8.321
Metric	millimetre	4.586
	centimetre	45.864
Imperial	inch	116.496
	foot	1 397.952

co-ordinates   identifiable points on a graph or matrix
which may be located by reference to stated
points on the horizontal and vertical axis
(*SEE* MATRIX STORE)

copperplate script   a group of typefaces based on
traditional 18th century engraved letters,
eg palace script
(CLASSIFICATION OF TYPE / BLOCK LETTER / *SEE* BRUSH SCRIPT)

abcdefghijklm

A B C D E

abcdefghijklmnopqrstuvwxyz

A B C D E F G H I J

ABCDEFGHIJKLM

abcdefghijklmnopqrstuvwxyz

copyfitting   the activity of estimating the amount of
space that a given text will occupy when the
typographic parameters are fixed (*SEE* PARAMETERS)

copyfitting program   a specific set of instructions,
in this book designed for use with a pocket

calculator, for solving *copyfitting* problems;
for single line, *bodytext* and *running text*
programs, see Part VI (*SEE* TYPEFACTOR)

FOR A single line of type
TO FIND The number of characters

KEYSTROKES	PARAMETERS	TEST
AC	typefactor	26.66
×	measure in picas	15
÷	typesize	10
=	calculator display shows the number of characters	40

copyright mark © (FOUNT/AMPERSAND/*SEE* REGISTERED MARK ®)
counter the white, or negative, space enclosed by
the strokes of characters (LINK/*SEE* CHARACTER)

counting keyboard in photocomposition systems a
keyboard at which the operator controls the *end
of line decisions*;
to this end the keyboard displays the cumulative
widths of each of the characters, calculated in
relative units, and as they are being typed;
when the number of characters approach the

PHOTOCOMPOSITION TYPOGRAPHY

specified measure a light is displayed or a
warning bell sounds whereupon the operator
must decide where to hyphenate if necessary;
when all of the copy is keyboarded it is then
stored on a tape along with the complete
typographic specification;
therefore in order to make changes to the stored
specification the entire copy may have to be re-
keyboarded

(HARDWARE/KEYBOARD/*SEE* NON-COUNTING KEYBOARD)

cpp   abbreviation for *characters per pica*

cps   abbreviation for *characters per second*

cpu   abbreviation for *central processing unit*

cross stroke   short horizontal stroke cutting through
the main stem of a character

(CHARACTER/STEM/*SEE* ASCENDER)

crossed stem   characters in which the *stems* overlap
and do not form an *apex* (CHARACTER/APEX/*SEE* BAR 2)

crt   abbreviation for *cathode ray tube*

c/sc   abbreviation for *caps* and *small caps*

cunieform   ancient inscriptions on clay tablets

(CLASSIFICATION OF TYPE/STYLUS/*SEE* GLYPHIC)

cursive   synonymous for *script*

cursor   moving dash or spot on a *visual display unit* to
show the operator the next point of input on the
visual display screen

(HARDWARE/PAGE MAKE-UP TERMINAL/*SEE* PHOTO UNIT)

cyclic store   here data is stored over a number of
quite separate cyclic tracks running parallel to
each other and in drums or disk form;
in this method data need not be entered in strict
sequence (as in a *serial store*) but may be read
across the tracks or segments and out of phase;
this facility is also known as *random access
memory*

(HARDWARE/MAGNETIC TAPE CASSETTE/*SEE* MAGNETIC DISK)

D

D abbreviation for *didot* (eg 14ptD)

dagger † second order reference mark
(FOUNT/ASTERISK/*SEE* DOUBLE DAGGER)

dash — (*SEE* EM DASH)

data fixed values operated upon by a computer but
not the program itself;
in computerised photocomposition one example
of data would be the *set width* of each character
held internally within the system (data also
should not be confused with information which
may be described as the result of operations
carried out on data by a computer, eg data such
as the set widths of characters may be
transformed into information such as the *measure*
of a given number of specified characters
(SOFTWARE/TRACE PARAMETERS/*SEE* DATABASE)

database a large store of fixed data held within the
computer, eg the set widths of characters or
rules for hyphenation and justification
(SOFTWARE/DATA/*SEE* K)

data carrier in the processing of data any medium
that may be used for the recording and storing of
data either by tape, disk or drum
(HARDWARE/DIRECT KEYBOARD/*SEE* SERIAL STORE)

dead matter type matter which has no further use
(*SEE* LIVE MATTER)

decimal an *integer* represented by a single number
from 0–9

decimal notation a number system in which
successive digit positions are represented by
successive powers of the radix 10
(NUMBER SYSTEMS/RADIX/*SEE* BINARY NOTATION)

definition in general, the degree of sharpness of a photographic reproduction on to a light sensitive paper, film or glass base;
in those photocomposition systems based on the principle of *character projection* individual characters are often designed with special *nicks* and *keys* which help to enhance definition
(HARDWARE/STABILIZATION PAPER/*SEE* OUTPUT RESOLUTION)

delete instruction on proof to remove redundant character, word or line of text
(*SEE* PROOF CORRECTION MARKS)

descender the parts of some *lower case* characters such as p, q, y which hang below the *baseline*
(CHARACTER/ASCENDER/*SEE* APEX)

pqrs

diacritical marks accents, dots and other linguistic signs used to notate the differing sounds of a character (*SEE* ACUTE)

diaeresis ë used in English over the second of two adjacent vowels to show that they are pronounced separately, eg Noël
(DIACRITICAL MARKS/CIRCUMFLEX/*SEE* DIPTHONG)

diagonal fraction (*SEE* FRACTION)

diazo (*SEE* OZALID PROOF)

didones BS equivalent to modern face
(BS/HUMANIST/*SEE* GARALDES)

Didot an old French typefoundry which in 1775 gave its name to a system of typographical measurement (*SEE* POINT)

digital computer   in comparison to *analog* systems it
is digital computers that are used exclusively in
the photocomposition of type;
digital computers operate on data which is
transformed into a sequence of coded numbers;
in most digital computer systems the method of
number representation is based on the system of
binary notation;
digital computers can store a vast amount of data,
operate at extremely high speeds and undertake
highly complex tasks
(HARDWARE/OFF-LINE/*SEE* PERIPHERAL UNIT)

digitisation   in photocomposition by character
formation the specification of an image as a
sequence of units capable of being processed
electronically in a computer's magnetic store as
simple yes/no or on/off alternatives (must not be
confused with *unitisation*)
(SOFTWARE/UNJUSTIFIED TAPE/*SEE* MATRIX STORE)

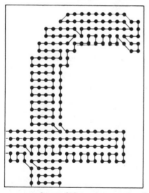 

examples of the character f digitised in lines and dots

dipthong æ œ   (DIACRITICAL MARKS/DIAERESIS/*SEE* ESZETT)

present language in

roducts are more ve

and they open up

characters digitised at 63 lines to the inch

beauty, variety and in

The first thing to rem

camera and that its fi

characters digitised at 125 lines to the inch

abcdefghijklmnopqrstuv

ABCDEFGHIJKLMN(

characters digitised at 166 lines to the inch

lmnopqrstuvwxyz£12

KLMNOPQRSTUVWXYZ

HIJKLMNOPQRST

mnopqrstuvwxyz£123

characters digitised at 1 000 lines to the inch

direct keyboard   operates directly into a
   photocomposition system driving the equipment
   directly and on command;
   no tape is produced from which the command
   might be transferred or corrected at some later
   stage (HARDWARE/BLIND KEYBOARD/SEE DATA CARRIER)

disc   not to be confused with *disk* (SEE FILM DISC)

discretionary justification   in this operation
   hyphenation is carried out manually by the
   keyboard operator. The computer uses
   whatever hyphenation is necessary to *justify*
   lines of type and disregarding the other
   hyphenation (SEE LOGIC JUSTIFICATION)

diskette   a smaller, single sided version of a
   magnetic disk;
   also known as a floppy disk and measures about
   6in square;
   when data is recorded on both sides of the
   diskette it may be known as either a flippy or a
   flippy-floppy
   (HARDWARE/MAGNETIC DISK/SEE MAGNETIC DRUM)

display size   typefaces large than 14pt
   (CLASSIFICATION OF TYPE/COMPOSITION SIZE/SEE HEADLINE TYPE)

dot matrix   any array in which a sequence of coded
   dots may be selected to form an image
   (SEE MATRIX PRINTER)

dot printer   synonymous with *matrix printer*

double dagger ‡   third order reference mark
   (FOUNT/DAGGER/SEE SECTION)

downstroke   heavy stroke of a letter originally
   produced by the directional movement of a pen
   (SEE THICKS AND THINS)

downtime   the period during which a
   photocomposition system is inoperable due to a
   machine fault (SEE REAL TIME)

drop cap   *upper case* character set in a larger

typesize and extending into the lines of type
below, with alignment along the *capital line*

DO WE NEED
Remember, 120
design by Frederic
old fellows that
our best ideas. But what do we

drop initial   (*SEE* DROP CAP)
drum   1) in computerised data (*SEE* MAGNETIC DRUM)
        2) in character assembly (*SEE* FILM DRUM)
dyeline   (*SEE* OZALID PROOF)

ear   the small stroke emerging from the right of the
        bowl of characters such as g and stem of r
        (CHARACTER/BOWL/*SEE* LOOP)

g g r r

editing terminal   synonymous with, but not so
accurate for *visual editing terminal*

Egyptian   *monoline* typeface of early 19th century
origin having unbracketed slab serifs

abcdefghijkl
ABCDEFGHIJ

abcdefghijklmnopq
ABCDEFGHIJKLM

abcdefghij
ABCDEFG

abcdefghijklmnopqr
ABCDEFGHIJKLM

electron beam in photocomposition by *character formation* a beam of electrons directed on to the phosphor coated surface of a *cathode ray tube*

elite typewriter the smaller of two standard *typewriter faces* and having 12 characters to the inch (SEE CHARACTER COUNT)

ellipses ... three full points set in a row and used to denote a pause in speech, suspended thought, or an omission in excerpted text
(FOUNT/BRACE/SEE REFERENCE MARKS)

em a variable typesetting dimension (derived from the M) and based on the square of a typesize, eg for 10pt type the em would be 10×10pt and for

48pt em

en $= \frac{1}{2}$ width of em

36pt em

24pt em above, 12pt em below

14pt type the em would then be 14 × 14pt
and so on;

the em is also known as a mutton;

in typesetting specifications dimensions are
usually specified as pica ems or 12pt ems
(TYPE MARK UP /M /*SEE* N)

em dash —   US term for *em rule*

em quad   clear white space being equal to the
square, or *em* of the typesize

em rule —   commonly referred to as a dash and
normally used to indicate an abrupt break in
speech or statements not essential to the meaning
of the sentence, eg;

this book is useful to the novice — and to the
experienced — designer (FOUNT /HYPHEN /*SEE* BRACKETS)

en   a variable typesetting dimension (derived from
the lower case n) and based on one half of the
width of the em;

therefore in 10pt type the en would be 10pt high
and 5pt wide, and so on;

to distinguish it from the em the en is often
referred to as a *nut* (TYPE MARK-UP /N /*SEE* QUAD)

en dash –   US term for *en rule*

endless tape   (*SEE* UNJUSTIFIED TAPE)

end of line decisions   (*SEE* HYPHENATION AND JUSTIFICATION)

en quad   clear white space equal to half of the *em* of
the typesize

en rule –   longer than the hyphen and normally used
to denote the words 'and' 'to', eg master–servant
relationship, London–Brighton car race
(FOUNT /HYPHEN /*SEE* EM RULE)

eszett ß   used in German to represent 'ss'
(DIACRITICAL MARKS /DIPTHONG /*SEE* ETH)

eth ð Ð   in Anglo-Saxon and Icelandic to represent
the soung 'th' as in thorn
(DIACRITICAL MARKS /ESZETT /*SEE* GRAVE)

exception dictionary   in this instance computers
programmed with a dictionary of hyphenated
words;
if the word to be hyphenated does not appear
in the dictionary then the computer program
will go on to break the word according to a
pre-programmed set of rules for hyphenation
(SOFTWARE/LOGIC JUSTIFICATION/*SEE* UNJUSTIFIED TAPE)

exclamation mark !   used to indicate strong feeling
such as surprise, irony, passion or joy;
always appears outside quotation marks
(FOUNT/QUESTION MARK/*SEE* HYPHEN)

expanded   one of many variants to the relative width
of a typeface (*SEE* TYPEFACE WIDTH)

family   synonymous for *family of type*
family of type   one typeface with all its variants of
weight, width, size, romans and italics
(TYPEFACE WEIGHT/*SEE* CLASSIFICATION OF TYPE)

fat face   a group of typefaces derived from *modern
face* letterforms;
contrast between the *thicks* and *thins* is extreme

figure   alternative typographic reference for the

individual numerals of a fount

(FOUNT /LIGATURE /*SEE* OLD STYLE FIGURES)

file   the organised collection of records such as
typesizes, corrections, measures, etc on the
magnetic store of a computerised
photocomposition system

(SOFTWARE /STORAGE /*SEE* RETRIEVAL)

film   the light sensitive photographic base which will
receive character assembly in the photo unit

(HARDWARE /OUTPUT MATERIAL /*SEE* NEGATIVE)

film advance   (*SEE* LINE FEED)

film composition   synonymous, but not so accurate,
for *photocomposition*;
in this sense it implies a system that can compose
setting on film only, whereas most modern
machines can compose type on film and paper

film disc   in photocomposition systems based on the
principle of *character projection*, an image
master in the form of a negative disc of film,
usually embedded in acrylic or glass (not to be
confused with disk)

(IMAGE MASTER /FILM STRIP /*SEE* SEGMENTED DISC)

film drum   a type of *image carrier* used in
photocomposition systems with the light source
located internally

filmsetting   synonymous, but not so accurate, for
photocomposition;
in this sense it implies a machine that outputs
setting on film only, whereas most modern
machines can output setting on film and paper

film strip   in photocomposition systems based on the
principle of *character projection*, an
image-master in the form of a negative strip of
film embedded usually in acrylic or glass

(IMAGE MASTER /*SEE* FILM DISC)

finial   (*SEE* SWASH)

first revise US term synonymous for *revised proof*

flash the release of a very brief interval of strong
light to expose a single character in
photocomposition systems based on the
principle of *character projection*;
where a character was not to be exposed the
instruction would be 'no flash'

flippy two-sided floppy disk (*SEE* DISKETTE)

floating accent `···` an accented sign separate from
the main character and known in US as a piece
accent (*SEE* DIACRITICAL MARKS)

floppy disk (*SEE* DISKETTE)

flow chart computers cannot function properly
unless the problems they are asked to solve
follow instructions which define in detail each
step of the solution;
the technique used for this purpose is called flow
charting;
the events recorded in a flow chart will record
the interconnexion between events of the same
type, through the means of standardised symbols
and connecting lines;
flow charts do not have to be written in the same
language as that of the computer program and
may also be known as logical trees, block
diagrams, or algorithms
(SOFTWARE/GIGO/*SEE* TRACE PROGRAM)

flush left (*SEE* RANGE)

font (*SEE* FOUNT)

foot one sided serif sitting on the baseline of
characters such as b, d (CHARACTER/BEAK/*SEE* SWASH)

foreign alphabets (*SEE* LATIN ALPHABET)

format 1) the dimensions of a layout or specified
sheet of typesetting;
2) the ability to record strings of commands
in the memory of a computer (*SEE* FILE)

FORTRAN   (*SEE* LANGUAGE)

fount   pronounced font. UK spelling as indexed here;
US spelling 'font';
the complete assembly of all elements
comprising a single typesize (*SEE* CHARACTER (2))

fount master   (*SEE* IMAGE MASTER)

founts per master   the number of single size
typefaces that one *image master* holds

fraction   1) a number which is less than the smallest
increment available, eg $\frac{1}{4}$ or 0.25
(INTEGER/*SEE* MIXED NUMBER)

2) diagonal fractions ($^3/_4$) are available
in four forms (*SEE* ADAPTABLE FRACTIONS)

full point .   the full point denotes the end of a
sentence. If also at the end of a quotation, it is
always placed within the quotation mark;
in US known as period
(FOUNT/SCRATCH COMMA/*SEE* COMMA)

full sized fraction   made from full sized numerals,
eg 3/4 (*SEE* ADAPTABLE FRACTIONS)

full stop .   equivalent of printers/designers term for
full point

galley proof   initial proof of typeset matter output
direct from the typesetting machine on long
strips of photographic paper;
usually supplied to the designer as photocopies
so that he/she might check that the type mark-up
has been followed
(PROOF CORRECTION MARKS/AUTHORS ALTERATIONS/*SEE* AUTHORS
PROOF)

ABCDEFGHIJK
LMNOPQRSTUV
WXYZ
abcdefghijklmnop
qrstuvwxyzß
1234567890
.,:;!¡?¿()[]«»*'''''°
&§£$%/†#@
–‒—×=+ aeilmorst
ÜÉÙÎĞŐŠÑŮŻÇ
üéùîğőšñůżç
ÆŒÅĄĘØĐĹĽŁ
æœåąęøďđłľťı

garaldes BS equivalent to *old face* (DIDONES/*SEE* BS)

garbage-in/garbage-out (gigo) because a computer
program cannot reason it depends entirely on
data supplied to it by human users;
therefore inaccurate data *input* will only result in
equally inaccurate *output* and this process is
called gigo (SOFTWARE/PROGRAM/*SEE* FLOWCHART)

geometrical sans serif a group of typefaces based
on Bauhaus principles and constructed of severe
geometric shapes having an apparently even line
thickness, eg Futura
(CLASSIFICATION OF TYPEFACES/SANS SERIF/*SEE* HUMANIST SANS SERIF)

abcdefghijkl
ABCDEFGHI
mnopqrstuv
JKLMNOPQ

gigo abbreviation for *garbage-in/garbage-out*
glass disc (*SEE* FILM DISC)
glyphic a group of typefaces having evolved from
chiselled letterforms
(CLASSIFICATION OF TYPE/CUNIEFORM/*SEE* CHANCERY ITALIC)

gothic 1) in US synonymous for *grotesque sans serif*
2) in UK synonymous for *black letter*

grave è used to signify that an otherwise mute
syllable should be sounded separately
(DIACRITICAL MARKS/ETH/*SEE* HACEK)

grotesque sans serif a group of typefaces
developed from early 19th century adaptations of
the modern face and retaining a hint of vertical
stress, eg Univers, Grotesque (also known in the
US as gothic)
(CLASSIFICATION OF TYPEFACES/HUMANIST SANS SERIF/*SEE* SLAB SERIF)

abcdefghij
ABCDEFG
klmnopqrs
HIJKLMN
tuvwxyz

haček č š (DIACRITICAL MARKS/GRAVE/SEE THORN)

handshaking when a *central processing unit* is linked
to an output device it may be that the former can
transmit information at a speed different to the
operating rate of the output device; in this case a
buffer is placed between the two to act as a
reservoir and the automatic signalling that then
takes place between them is therefore called
handshaking

hanging indent (SEE REVERSE INDENT)

hanging punctuation punctuation marks that are
located in the margin of the text and not ranged
with the column
(REVERSE INDENT/SEE PROOF CORRECTION MARKS)

hard copy typewritten duplicate of input produced
alongside the magnetic tape/disk and used to
check errors before the tape is committed to
character assembly in the photo unit
(HARDWARE/LPM/SEE LINE PRINTER)

hardware a term used to identify all those items of
actual operating equipment, eg the keyboard,
the computer, the photo unit
(PHOTOCOMPOSITION/COMPUTERISED PHOTOCOMPOSITION/
SEE SOFTWARE)

hard wired a photocomposition system in which
permanently pre-wired circuit boards are used
to carry out a specific data processing or
photocomposition operation;
they cannot therefore be re-programmed
(SEE PROGRAM)

headline type regardless of size, but because of its
style, type that is unsuitable for setting large

quantities as text and is therefore restricted to headings

(CLASSIFICATION OF TYPE/DISPLAY SIZE/*SEE* TYPEFACE WIDTH)

heavy synonymous for *bold face* (*SEE* TYPEFACE WEIGHT)

h/j abbreviation for *hyphenation and justification*

horizontal fraction as here $\frac{3}{4}$ (*SEE* PIECE FRACTION)

house corrections synonymous for *printers errors*

humanist BS equivalent to *venetian face*
(BS/LINEALE/*SEE* DIDONES)

humanist sans serif a group of typefaces having the proportions of the romans and venetians and usually retaining the old style **a** and **g**, eg Gill Sans
(CLASSIFICATION OF TYPEFACES/GEOMETRICAL SANS SERIF/ *SEE* GROTESQUE SANS SERIF)

abcdefghijkl
ABCDEFGHI
mnopqrstuv
JKLMNOPQ
wxyz

hyphen - used to connect the two parts of a
compound word as in Anglo-American or to
connect the parts of a word divided at the end of
a line of typesetting
(FOUNT/EXCLAMATION MARK/*SEE* EN RULE)

hyphenation in photocomposition systems the
hyphenation of words may be of four kinds
1) *hyphenless justification*
2) *discretionary justification*
3) *logic justification*
4) *exception dictionary*

hyphenation and justification (h/j) some
computers are programmed to carry out end of
line decisions automatically so that columns of
type may be justified to right and left;
the spacing of letters and words to justify
columns is entered into the computer program
by the operator via a *non-counting keyboard*
(SOFTWARE/MERGING/*SEE* LOGIC JUSTIFICATION)

hyphenless justification the ability of photocomposition systems to justify bodytext so that
words/characters within the measure are spaced
to ensure that words at the end of line remain
unbroken (LAYOUT/JUSTIFY/*SEE* RAGGED)

idiot tape (*SEE* UNJUSTIFIED TAPE)
image carrier a mechanical device capable of
holding more than one negative film image
master for character projection
(HARDWARE/IMAGE MASTER/*SEE* CHARACTER EXPOSURE)
image master (also referred to as typemaster,

Normal
Condense
Expand
Italicise
Backslant
Stagger

character deformations produced from a single digital
image master

fountmaster, character grid, matrix) in photocomposition systems based on the principle of character projection the image master will contain a hard negative film image of the complete fount;

this image may take the form of a *film strip* or *film disc*;

in those other photocomposition systems based on the principle of character formation the image master is stored digitally in the *computer* as a series of electronic impulses;

the advantage of digital image masters is the ability to moderate the character shape electronically by the computer and from a single image master, see previous page;

in *character projection* a different image master is required for every variation to the standard fount (HARDWARE/CHARACTER FORMATION/*SEE* IMAGE CARRIER)

imperial system   little used for typographic calculations and based on the inch which is divisible into numerous fractions

1 inch = 72 Anglo-American points
12 inches = 1 foot

(MEASURING SYSTEMS/INCREMENTS/*SEE* AGATE LINE)

inch (in)   increment in the *imperial system* of measurement

increment for interline spacing   a term used in the tables for photocomposition systems, Part III of this book, to describe the units of space that can be added or subtracted between lines of type and specified in *points* or sub-divisions of the *point*

increment for typesize increase   a term used in the tables for photocomposition systems, Part III of this book, to identify the range of typesizes between the minimum and maximum typesizes

increments   in any measuring system the units by

which dimensions may be calculated
(SEE POINT SYSTEM/UNIT SYSTEM/METRIC SYSTEM/IMPERIAL
SYSTEM/CONVERSION TABLES)

indent a common method of indicating paragraphs
by leaving a blank space at the beginning of a
line (SEE REVERSE INDENT)

inferior characters small characters set to appear
near the baseline of a typesize, eg H_2O;
also known as sub-scripts
(FOUNT/SUPERIOR CHARACTERS/SEE LIGATURE)

informal script synonymous for *script*

inline a group of typefaces having white lines on the
black printing surface of the character
(CLASSIFICATION OF TYPE/OUTLINE/SEE SHADOW)

input expression used to denote any information or
instructions to be processed. May also be used as
a verb (SEE GIGO)

insert instruction on proof to add missing characters,
words or lines of text (SEE PROOF CORRECTION MARKS)

integer any number comprised of whole *increments*,
eg 2 5 6 7 (SEE FRACTION)

intelligent terminal any source of input, such as
a keyboard, which is capable of being
programmed and may perform certain
commands such as word-break decisions
independently of the main computer program
(HARDWARE/PERIPHERAL UNIT/SEE COMPATIBILITY)

interface a device which enables two items of
hardware to communicate with each other
(SEE SERIAL INTERFACE)

interline spacing the creation of non-printing white

space between lines of type and (unlike letter
spacing) specified in standard increments of
points or divisions of the point;
interline spacing may also be referred to as line
spacing and leading

(TYPE MARK-UP/KERNING/*SEE* SET SOLID)

inverted commas   (*SEE* QUOTATION MARKS)

ionic   a group of typefaces from the mid 19th century
having bracketed slab serifs and *modern face*
letterforms and used a great deal in newspapers

(BRUSH SCRIPT/*SEE* CLASSIFICATION OF TYPE)

ABCDEFGHIJKLMNOP QRSTUVWXYZabcdefg hijklmnopqrstuvwxyz 1234567890(?)&.,;:!%

italic   in general those typefaces which slope to the
right, in particular a typestyle having evolved
from *chancery script*

(CLASSIFICATION OF TYPE/ROMAN/*SEE* BACKSLANT)

geschätzt. Im Schriftenatelier Münc
zwölf Zentimetern neu gezeichnet.
Schriftscheiben das Optimale an
alität des Einzelzeichens im Belicht
ruhende, nicht rotierende Schriftsch
bunden mit Präzisions-Chromglass

PHOTOCOMPOSITION TYPOGRAPHY

justify   bodytext, in which all lines have been made to
an equal measure and therefore line up, or range,
vertically to both left and right of the column
(LAYOUT /MAXIMUM MEASURE /*SEE* HYPHENLESS JUSTIFICATION)

rminée avec précision. Tous les caractères du
même corps ont des capitales d'une hauteur
identique, indépendamment de la hauteur d
es bas de casse sans jambage. Dans la comp
osition plomb, ainsi que dans certains systè
mes de photocomposition, la hauteur des ca
pitales, varie souvent d'un caractère à l'autr
e. Pour déterminer la force de corps de nos c
aractères, nous avons mis au point une régl
ette de hauteur d'œil transparente. On cher

justifying keyboard   same as *counting keyboard*

k   abbreviation for 1 000;
the capacity of a computer store is usually
expressed as a number which is followed by k,
ie thousands of units of *binary* data
(SOFTWARE /DATABASE /*SEE* STORAGE)

kcs   abbreviation for a thousand characters per
second (*SEE* CPS)

kerning   the adjustment of space between individual letters so that the part of one extends over the body of another;
unlike letterspacing, which is normally a blanket specification applying to all letterpairs and regardless of their individual characteristics, kerning is a selective process and some computers are programmed to perform this process automatically; kerning pairs below

(TYPE MARK-UP/PLUS LETTERSPACING/*SEE* INTERLINE SPACING)

AC AL AN AO AT AV AW AY

Av Aw ac af ao at au av

aw ax ay

CA CO CT CY Co Ce

DY du

ew ex ey

FA FG FO F, F. Fa Fe Fo Fu

GY

KE KO ke ko ku

LA LI LL LO LS LT LV LW LY

Ma mu

NT nu

OA OT OV OW OY

PA PE PO PR P, P. Pa Pe Po Pr
Qu
RA RO RV RY ra rc re ro
SA ST SY sys st
TA TC TE TO TS TW TY T, T.
Ta Te To Tr Tu Tw Ty
VA VO VY V, V. Va Ve Vo
WA WO WV WY W, W. Wa We
Wh Wi Wo Wr wa we w, w.
YA YO YS Y, Y. Ya Ye Yo
ya ye yo ys y, y.
ZA

key   in photocomposition based on the system of
character projection, a key shaped indent is left
out of the corners of characters which, when
exposed, fills in to give a sharp, square edge
(NICK /*SEE* DEFINITION)

keyboard   the part of a photocomposition machine
similar to a typewriter and at which the operator
may sit and type in copy to be set
(PHOTOCOMPOSITION /HARDWARE /*SEE* COUNTING KEYBOARD)

key in   the addition of data and instructions to a
computerised photocomposition system via its
keyboard

keyword index (kwic/kwoc)   in data retrieval the
significant word in a title which may be used
to extract the related data from a computers
magnetic store;
keywords can be described as in context with the
rest of the title (kwic), or as outside of it (kwoc)
(SOFTWARE/RETRIEVAL/*SEE* MNEMONIC CODING)

kill   instruction to operator of a computerised
photocomposition system to delete erroneous or
unwanted copy before it proceeds to the photo
unit for output (DEAD MATTER/LIVE MATTER/*SEE* SOFTWARE)

kph   abbreviation for *keystrokes per hour* (*SEE* KEYBOARD)

kwic/kwoc   abbreviations for 'keyword in context'
and 'keyword out of context' (*SEE* KEYWORD INDEX)

language   for men to communicate with computers
several machine languages have been devised;
in high level computer languages the coded
instructions will still make some sort of sense to
someone who has not learned the language
whereas in low level languages this is not the case;
several computer languages are as follows:
ALGOL (ALGOrithmic Language)
COBOL (COmmon Business Orientated Language)
FORTRAN (FORmula TRANslator)
PL/1 (Programming Language/one)
BASIC (Beginners All-purpose Symbolic
Instruction Code)
(PHOTOCOMPOSITION/SOFTWARE/*SEE* PROGRAM)

large fractions   made from full sized numerals, eg 3/4
(*SEE* ADAPTABLE FRACTIONS)

laser   a specially treated and unique form of light
source composed of a single fine beam of light;
each side of this beam is, and will remain,
parallel to the other;
a laser beam is therefore called coherent light
and is unlike any other light source in which the
beams will scatter in random array, and are
therefore called non-coherent light
(*SEE* CHARACTER EXPOSURE)

Latin   1) serifs – a style of typeface having triangular
serifs (BRACKETED SERIF /*SEE* SLAB SERIF)

ABCDEFGHIJKLMNOPQR
STUVWXYZabcdefghijklm
nopqrstuvwxyz

2) alphabet – those alphabets used in the
western world (*SEE* DIACRITICAL MARKS)

layout   a plan designed to show the arrangement of
type within a given area (*SEE* RUN-AROUND)

lc   abbreviation for *lower case*

leading   in metal typesetting the addition of thin strips
of non-printing lead to create additional white
space between lines of type (*SEE* INTERLINE SPACING)

lens turret   an assembly of different optical lenses
through which a single character image may be
projected with each lens providing an
enlargement or reduction to the original
character size (*SEE* CHARACTER EXPOSURE)

letter   1) to letter; the art of rendering text by hand as
in calligraphy;
2) handwritten sign expressing a sound of
speech (*SEE* CHARACTER)

letterfit   in the composition of type the quality of the space between the individual characters (not to be confused with *letterspacing* which simply refers to the amount of space between letters) eg the letterfit is good

letterspacing   the addition of white space between characters in very fine increments and based on the divisions of the em with the increments known as *relative units*
(TYPE MARK-UP/WORDSPACE/*SEE* NORMAL LETTERSPACING)

'Legibility, in practice, amounts simply to what one is accustomed

'Legibility, in practice, amounts simply to what one is

'Legibility in practice, amounts simply to what one

'Legibility, in practice, amounts simply to what

letterstroke   individual linear element of a handwritten letter (*SEE* CHARACTER STROKE)

ligature   two or more characters physically linked together in a single unit
(FOUNT/INFERIOR CHARACTERS/*SEE* FIGURE)

lightface   one of the many variants to the relative blackness of a typeface (*SEE* TYPEFACE WEIGHT)

lineale   BS equivalent to sans serif (BS/*SEE* HUMANIST)

line-endless tape   (*SEE* UNJUSTIFIED TAPE)

line feed   the amount by which photocomposition machines advance the paper or film from line to line and may also be referred to as film advance
(*SEE* INTERLINE SPACING)

line-for-line   a typographic specification for bodytext where each line is calculated and specified separately (*SEE* RUN-AROUND)

line increment   the smallest increment by which *interline spacing* may be added or subtracted between lines of type

line length   (*SEE* MEASURE)

line printer   a computer output device used to produce typewritten *hardcopy* for proof-reading with setting speeds of around 500–2 000 *lpm*
(HARDWARE / HARDCOPY / *SEE* BI-DIRECTIONAL LINE PRINTER)

linespacing   (*SEE* INTERLINE SPACING)

lining figures   numerals consistently equal to the capital height of the fount;
also known as ranging figures
(FOUNT / OLD STYLE FIGURES / *SEE* ADAPTABLE FRACTIONS)

AB123456789

link   stroke connecting the bowl and loop of the letter g (CHARACTER / LOOP / *SEE* COUNTER)

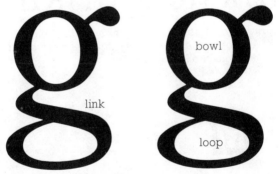

live matter   type matter which is to be held for re-use
(DEAD MATTER / *SEE* KILL)

logical tree   (*SEE* FLOW CHART)

logic justification   in this instance computers programmed with a specific set of rules for hyphenation;

all those words to which the rules can be applied are hyphenated accordingly;
all of those words for which the rules do not apply are left un-hyphenated and the computer program then goes on to automatically adjust letter and word spacing to justify the line (SOFTWARE/HYPHENATION AND JUSTIFICATION/*SEE* EXCEPTION DICTIONARY)

loop rounded form not of the formal character of a bowl as in the lower part of the letter g (CHARACTER/EAR/*SEE* LINK)

lower case (lc) the small letters of a fount, also known as miniscules (FOUNT/UPPER CASE/*SEE* SMALL CAPITALS)

abcdefghijklm

lpm abbreviation meaning the speed at which a photo unit can perform *character assembly* and calculated in lines per minute (HARDWARE/CPS/*SEE* HARD COPY)

m in the metric system abbreviation for *metre*
M in typography the capital letter M is usually the widest letter in a *fount* and in early founts it was normally cast on a square body (TYPE MARK-UP/SPACING/*SEE* EM)

macron ē horizontal line over a vowel indicating that it is long (BREVE/*SEE* DIACRITICAL MARKS)

magnetic disk   a storage device comprising a
     number of flat circular plates having a number of
     separate cyclic tracks on each side
     (HARDWARE/CYCLIC STORE/*SEE* DISKETTE)

magnetic drum   a cyclic storage device comprising
     a cylinder around the surface of which are a
     number of parallel recording tracks;
     as the drum rotates data may be extracted from
     any of the tracks, and out of phase or sequence
     (HARDWARE/DISKETTE/*SEE* READ–WRITE HEAD)

magnetic memory   synonymous with *magnetic store*

magnetic reel tape   an open-ended tape storage
     device, consisting of one reel usually about $10\frac{1}{2}$in
     diameter and on which about 2 400 feet of $\frac{1}{2}$in
     wide magnetic tape is wound;
     in operation, tape is wound between two reels
     (HARDWARE/MAGNETIC STORE/*SEE* MAGNETIC TAPE CASSETTE)

magnetic store   any data carrier or storage device
     which, in order to operate, uses the principle of
     electro-magnetism;
     magnetic stores permit a much greater density of
     data to be stored which may also be erased and
     re-used (HARDWARE/PERFORATOR/*SEE* MAGNETIC REEL TAPE)

magnetic tape cassette   a tape storage device
     consisting of a magnetic tape enclosed within a
     sealed plastic container measuring approximately
     $4 \times 2\frac{1}{2}$in (HARDWARE/MAGNETIC REEL TAPE/*SEE* CYCLIC STORE)

majuscules   (*SEE* UPPER CASE)

marching display unit   one type of *vdu* in which a
     narrow display is attached to a *keyboard*;
     only one line is displayed at a time and only the
     last 30–40 characters as they are input via the
     keyboard;
     the screen usually displays red or white
     characters on a black background
     (HARDWARE/REVERSE FIELD VDU/*SEE* CATHODE RAY TUBE)

marked proof   synonymous for *revised proof*

mark-up   *(SEE* TYPE MARK-UP)

master proof   galley or page proof in which the printers errors and authors alterations have been combined

(PROOF CORRECTION MARKS/AUTHORS PROOF/*SEE* REVISED PROOF)

matrice   alternative but, in photocomposition, less frequent spelling for *matrix*

matrix   a rectangular table or array of numbers in which an isolated location may be identified by the use of *co-ordinates* *(SEE* CO-ORDINATES)

matrix printer   a class of line printer in which the characters are formed from a dot-matrix; also known as needle printer, stylus printer or dot printer

(HARDWARE/BI-DIRECTIONAL PRINTER/*SEE* BARREL PRINTER

matrix store   for a numerically stored, digitised image, where any particular location might be identified by the use of co-ordinates

(SOFTWARE/DIGITISATION/*SEE* SCANNING)

maximum interline spacing   a term used in the tables for photocomposition systems, Part III of this book, to describe the maximum number of *points* and subdivisions of the point that may be added between lines of type to create white space

maximum measure   1) in bodytext where lines are of varying lengths the maximum measure refers to the length of the longest line

2) the longest possible line of type that a photocomposition system can set – as used in the tables for photocomposition systems, Part III of this book (LAYOUT/MEASURE/*SEE* JUSTIFY)

maximum typesize   a term used in the tables for photocomposition systems, Part III of this book, to identify the largest typesize in points that a specified system can set

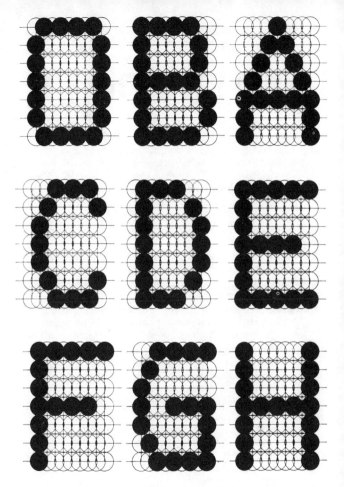

example of letters stored on a *dot matrix*

mean line an imaginary line running along the tops of lower case characters without ascenders
(MEASURING TYPE/CAPITAL LINE/*SEE* X-HEIGHT)

mnopqrs

measure in single lines of type or in bodytext, the length of the line or column width, usually specified in *picas* or *pica ems*
(LAYOUT/BODYTEXT/*SEE* MAXIMUM MEASURE)

measuring systems pre-determined systems by which dimensions can be calculated and recorded according to specific rules
(*SEE* INCREMENTS/CONVERSION TABLES)

measuring type (*SEE* TYPESIZE)

medium in the classification of typeface variants, the relative blackness of a fount (*SEE* TYPEFACE WEIGHT)

memory the internal information store of a machine used for data processing (*SEE* MAGNETIC STORE)

merging in computerised photocomposition systems two magnetic data stores one of which contains corrections whereas the other does not; each line of text is numbered so that the amended data may be merged with the original data to form a single corrected master instruction tape
(SOFTWARE/OCR/*SEE* HYPHENATION AND JUSTIFICATION)

metric system a decimal system of measurement developed in France in 1790; this system is used by some typesetting manufacturers for typographic specifications

millimetre (mm) smallest increment in the metric system of measurement and equal to 2.835 Anglo-American points
(MEASURING SYSTEMS/METRIC SYSTEM/*SEE* CENTIMETRE)

minimum typesize   a term used in the tables for
photocomposition systems, Part III of this book to
identify the smallest typesize in points that a
specified system can set.

miniscules   *(SEE* LOWER CASE*)*

minus leading   *(SEE* MINUS INTERLINE SPACING*)*

minus letterspacing   the tightening up of white
space between letters by the subtraction of
relative units from the normal set width of
characters, eg -3 units letter and word spacing
(TYPE MARK-UP/NORMAL LETTERSPACING/*SEE* LETTERSPACING)

mit   abbreviation for *master instruction tape*

mixed number   a number consisting of an integral
part and a fraction part, eg $10\frac{1}{2}$ or 10.5
(INTEGER/*SEE* NUMBER SYSTEMS)

mm   abbreviation for *millimetre*

mnemonic coding   in data storage and retrieval a
symbolic coding easier to remember than the
numeric code of machine systems;
for example the typeface Melior may be
represented as ME
(SOFTWARE/KEYWORD INDEX/*SEE* READ ONLY MEMORY)

modem   this, via a serial interface, connects a
computer to the telephone system permitting two
computers having modems to exchange
information *(SEE* INTERFACE*)*

moderns   a group of serif typefaces dating from the
late 18th century and showing little evidence of
their calligraphic origins;
the stress is vertical and the serifs are hairline
with horizontals having slight or no bracketing;
capitals are usually equal to the *ascender* height;
the serif at the foot of the b is no longer slanted
but horizontal to the baseline (uncharacteristic of
calligraphy). Contrast to the *thicks* and *thins* has
greatly increased and an extreme case is *fat face*;

typeface examples are Bodoni, Waulbaum, Scotch roman, Modern extended <small>(CLASSIFICATION OF TYPEFACES / VENETIANS AND OLD FACES / SEE TRANSITIONAL)</small>

abcdefghij
ABCDEF

abcdefghijklm
ABCDEFGHIJ

abcdefghijklmnop
ABCDEFGHIJKL

monoline   either a *sans serif* or *slab serif* typeface in which all stroke widths appear to be equal
<small>(CLASSIFICATION OF TYPE / BACKSLANT / SEE OUTLINE)</small>

mutt   abbreviation for *mutton*

mutton   <small>(SEE EM)</small>

n the width of the lower case 'n' in any fount
approximates to the average width of all
characters in the fount;
for this reason bodytext is calculated in the
average character width and referred to as the
en, eg how many ens does the copy make?
(TYPE MARK-UP/EM/*SEE* EN)

needle printer synonymous with *matrix printer*

negative type of photographic reproduction on
paper, film or glass in which the black and white
areas are reversed from those in the original
(HARDWARE/FILM/*SEE* POSITIVE)

negative interline spacing the subtraction of white
space between lines of type to produce an
interval less than the specified typesize;
less satisfactory terms are minus linespacing
and minus leading
(TYPE MARK-UP/SET SOLID/*SEE* WHITE LINE)

nick in photocomposition based on the system of
character projection, an extra hairline serif on
the corners of characters which disappears on
exposure, leaving a sharp, square corner (*SEE* KEY)

no flash (*SEE* FLASH)

non-coherent term applied to a light source in which
the emitted beams of light scatter in random
array (*SEE* COHERENT)

non-counting keyboard in computerised
photocomposition systems it is the computer, not
the operator, which makes *end of line decisions*;
in this case the keyboard gives the operator no
indication of his position within the line leaving
him free to type continuously thereby saving time;

in non-counting keyboards the typographic
specification has to be added after the straight
copy has been recorded on tape;
therefore, with this system one tape can be used
to make numerous alterations to the type
specification without the necessity of
re-keyboarding
(HARDWARE/COUNTING KEYBOARD/SEE BLIND KEYBOARD)

non-justifying keyboard   synonymous with
non-counting keyboard

non-ligning figures   (SEE OLD STYLE FIGURES)

normal letterspacing   the spacing of letters based
solely on the *set width* of the character which
itself includes additional units over and above
the designed width of the character
(TYPE MARK-UP/LETTERSPACING/SEE MINUS LETTERSPACING)

example of normal letterspacing

The breeding habitat is
rocky coast with offshore

example of modified letterspacing

The breeding habitat is
rocky coast with offshore

np   abbreviation for new paragraph
(SEE PROOF CORRECTION MARKS)

number of tab positions   (SEE TABULAR FACILITY)

number systems   any system for representing
numeric values or quantities (SEE POSITIONAL NOTATION)

numerals   (SEE ARABIC NUMERALS/FIGURE)

nut   (SEE EN)

oblique stroke / (SEE SOLIDUS)

ocr abbreviation for *optical character recognition*

OCR-B the name of a typeface designed by Adrian Frutiger and suitable for *ocr* systems

off-line any input or output device not connected directly to the computer nor under the control of its program (HARDWARE/ON-LINE/SEE DIGITAL COMPUTER)

old English in UK same as *black letter* (SEE TEXT TYPE)

old face (SEE VENETIANS AND OLD FACES)

old style US reference to *old face*
(SEE VENETIANS AND OLD FACES)

old style figures numerals which vary in size having ascenders and descenders;
also known as non-ligning figures
(FOUNT/FIGURE/SEE LINING FIGURES)

X1234567890

on-line any input or output devices connected directly to the computer and under the control of its program (HARDWARE/STAND-ALONE/SEE OFF-LINE)

optical character recognition (ocr) the ability of some computerised photocomposition systems to input data by recognising printed characters via a light sensing scanning device;
this method eliminates one stage of input where the original copy would otherwise have to be *keyboarded* by an operator
(SOFTWARE/REAL TIME/SEE MERGING)

ordinal number (SEE CARDINAL NUMBERS)

outline   characters which appear white with a black
outline (CLASSIFICATION OF TYPE / MONOLINE / SEE INLINE)

Typeface

output   in photocomposition systems;
1) results produced by the computer in either
paper tape or magnetic form
2) characters that have been assembled on to a
light sensitive base in the photo unit

output material   the light sensitive base, ie paper or
film, on to which a photo unit performs character
assembly;
as the generating light source moves over the
material it is also wound vertically in a roll to
facilitate the beginning of each new line;
this is called the *line feed*;
output material also comes in various widths
depending on the manufacturer (for details refer
to the photocomposition systems tables in Part III
of this book) (HARDWARE / CHARACTER EXPOSURE / SEE FILM)

output on film/paper   (SEE OUTPUT MATERIAL)

output resolution   the ability of a photo unit to
produce characters having a high definition,
eg in *character projection* output resolution is
governed by the intensity of the light flash and
the speed at which the image carrier moves
during character assembly;
however, in *character formation* the output
resolution is determined by the number of lines
per inch or millimetre at which the tracking *laser*
or *electron beam* can scan;
the greater the output resolution the better the

definition (HARDWARE /DEFINITION /*SEE* CPS)

Ozalid proof   brand name for a class of photographic
proofs made from machine film and before
platemaking, in which the image is made visible
by exposure to evaporating ammonia;
known alternatively as, blue-line, blueprints,
blues, brown print, diazo, vapour diazo, dyeline
and van dyke

(PROOF CORRECTION MARKS/PAGE PROOFS/*SEE* TYPE MARK-UP)

page make-up terminal   a visual display unit which
allows the operator to see keyboarded copy
made up as whole page;
some terminals offer a facsimile of the typestyle
and others an approximation

(HARDWARE /SCROLLING FACILITY /*SEE* CURSOR)

page view terminal (pvt)   synonymous with *page
make-up terminal*

page proofs   proofs showing original galley proofs
made up in page form and correctly positioned;
page proofs incorporate the original typesetting
plus additional line or half-tone work

(PROOF CORRECTION MARKS /REVISED PROOF /*SEE* OZALID PROOF)

paper/film widths   the light sensitive base, whether
paper or film used by photocomposition systems
comes in a variety of widths;
it is often more cost effective to choose a width of
output material near to the maximum measure;
the tables for photocomposition systems, Part III
of this book, specifies paper /film widths in
millimetres

paper tape   a strip of paper usually about 1 in wide
and on which data is recorded by unique
configurations of punched holes;
because the holes are permanent the tape cannot
be re-used and to make revisions and
corrections a new tape must be punched·
(HARDWARE /SERIAL STORE /*SEE* PERFORATOR)

para   abbreviation for paragraph
(*SEE* PROOF CORRECTION MARKS)

paragraph ¶   sixth order reference mark
(FOUNT /PARALLEL /*SEE* PI CHARACTERS)

parallel ‖   fifth order reference mark
(FOUNT /SECTION /*SEE* PARAGRAPH)

parallel interface   a device which allows characters
to be transmitted in batches down a multi-cored
cable and between two items of hardware but
only over short distances (*SEE* MODEM)

parameters   a set of variable quantities given fixed
values in order to carry out a specific calculation,
eg typesize, interline spacing, etc
(SOFTWARE /TRACE PROGRAM /*SEE* TRACE PARAMETERS)

parenthesis   (*SEE* BRACKETS)

pe   abbreviation for printers error, a US term the UK
equivalent of which is *authors alteration* (aa)

peculiar   (*SEE* PI CHARACTER)

PE paper   synonymous with *resin coated paper*

perforator   in photocomposition a keyboard unit
which also produces a punched paper tape
(HARDWARE /PAPER TAPE /*SEE* MAGNETIC STORE)

period .   US term for *full point*

peripheral unit   all those pieces of hardware which
are not part of the computer itself but are
operated by commands from it, eg magnetic
disk, photo unit, etc
(HARDWARE /DIGITAL COMPUTER /*SEE* INTELLIGENT TERMINAL)

phosphor   fluorescent substance used to coat the

inside surface of a *cathode ray* display unit and energised by a beam of electrons

photocomposition the most adequate term for all those systems of typesetting by photographic means utilising a *keyboard* for the input and a *photo unit* for the output
(SEE COMPUTERISED PHOTOCOMPOSITION)

photo-mechanical transfer (pmt) an instant form of line print which may be used for artwork

photosetting a vague term used to cover all those machines producing reproduction proofs of lettering by photographic means
(SEE PHOTOCOMPOSITION)

phototypesetting synonymous with *photocomposition*

photo unit the output component of a photocomposition system which *resolves* and produces the character assembly by projecting a light source on to light sensitive film or paper
(HARDWARE/CURSOR/SEE CHARACTER ASSEMBLY)

pi π the sixteenth letter of the Greek alphabet and mathematical symbol for the ratio of the circumference of a circle to the diameter, approximately 3.14159 (SEE PI CHARACTERS)

pica as a standard typographic unit one pica is equal to 12 Anglo-American points;
there are approximately 6 picas, or 72 points, to the inch (MEASURING SYSTEMS/POINT/SEE CICERO)

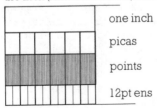

one inch

picas

points

12pt ens

pica typewriter larger of two standard *typewriter faces* and having 10 characters to the inch
(*SEE* CHARACTER COUNT)

pi characters (also known as sorts, pi founts, peculiars) special characters not normally present in a complete type fount, eg mathematical signs, reference marks, *diacritical marks*, symbols, etc
(FOUNT/PARAGRAPH/*SEE* AMPERSAND)

pie correct pronunciation but wrong spelling for *pi*
piece accent (*SEE* FLOATING ACCENT)
piece fraction small fractions made up from two pieces with the nominator and diagonal as one character (3/) and the denominator as the second (4), eg 3/4;
also known as split fraction
(FRACTIONS/CASE FRACTION/*SEE* QUOTATION MARKS)

pi facility the ability of mechanical typesetting systems to incorporate *pi characters*
pi founts (*SEE* PI CHARACTERS)
pi positions in some photocomposition systems blank spaces are left in regular *founts* so that the designer may insert special symbols or signs of his own design, or from the systems stock library of *pi characters*
PL/1 (*SEE* LANGUAGE)
plus letterspacing the loosening up of white space between letters by the addition of *relative units* to

PHOTOCOMPOSITION TYPOGRAPHY

the normal *set width* of characters, eg +3 units
letterspacing
(TYPE MARK-UP /MINUS LETTERSPACING /*SEE* KERNING)

pmt abbreviation for *photo-mechanical transfer*;
must not be confused with page make-up
terminal

point (pt) 1) Anglo-American point – smallest whole
typographic increment used in Anglo-American
countries with one such point equal to 0.35136mm
or 0.0138in
2) didot point – used in most European
countries with one point equal to 0.376mm or
0.015in, usually written as 1ptD
(MEASURING SYSTEMS /POINT SYSTEM /*SEE* PICA)

point size the measure used to define any given
typesize and calculated in *points*

point system a system of measurement devised
exclusively for typographic calculations
(MEASURING SYSTEMS /INCREMENTS /*SEE* POINT)

positional notation a form of number system in
which a given quantity is represented by a set of
digits so that both the position of the digit within
the set as well as its value is of importance, eg 192
or 219 in decimal notation (NUMBER SYSTEMS /*SEE* RADIX)

positive type of photographic reproduction on
paper, film or glass in which the black and white
areas correspond to those of the original
(HARDWARE /NEGATIVE /*SEE* RIGHT-READING)

pothook the curved terminal on some characters,
mostly in italics (CHARACTER /SPUR /*SEE* BOWL)

prelims/postlims those pages not occupied by the
main body of text, eg half title, title, imprint,
dedication, preface, foreword,
acknowledgements, contents, list of illustrations,
appendices, authors notes, glossary,
bibliography, index, etc

printer   an output device which converts data stored in a coded form into printed copy (*SEE* LINE PRINTER)

printers error (pe)   marked on proofs to signify those mistakes made by the typesetter;
is used more frequently in US
(PROOF CORRECTION MARKS/PRINTERS READER/*SEE* AUTHORS ALTERATIONS)

printers marks   (*SEE* PROOF CORRECTION MARKS)

printers reader   a person employed by the typesetter to correct proofs before they are sent to the client
(PROOF CORRECTION MARKS/PROOF/*SEE* PRINTERS ERROR)

printout   a general term for the output produced by a *line printer* (*SEE* HARD COPY)

program   the process by which a set of instructions is produced for a computer to make it perform a specific set of operations;
the instructions ultimately obeyed by the computer are numerical codes often, but not always, based on the yes/no binary system;
most computer programs are capable of revision and change, but those photocomposition systems having permanently pre-wired circuit boards are called hard wired (SOFTWARE/LANGUAGE/*SEE* GIGO)

proof   initial trial copy of typeset matter for correction and approval
(PROOF CORRECTION MARKS/*SEE* PRINTERS READER)

proof correction marks   a set of signs agreed by the British Standards Institute for use in the preparation of copy and the marking of proofs
(*SEE* PROOF)

pt   abbreviation for *point*

punched tape   synonymous for *paper tape*

punctuation marks   (*SEE* QUOTATION MARKS)

put down   instruction on proof to change caps to lower case (*SEE* PROOF CORRECTION MARKS)

Proof Correction Marks

For further reading on proof correction please refer to the Bibliography

Explanation	Marginal mark	Textual mark
Delete	⌐	Typographic design
Take in	⋏ design	Typographic ⋏
Set in upper-case	≡ u.c.	typographic design
Set in lower-case	≠ l.c.	Typographic DESIGN
Set in small capitals	≡ s.c.	Typographic DESIGN
Set in bold	∿ bld.	Typographic **design**
Set in italic	⫽ ital.	Typographic *design*
Set in roman	⫽ rom.	*Typographic* design
Leave as it is	stet ✓	Typographic design
Reposition	⌐	Typographic design
Wrong fount	⊗ wf.	Typographic design
Battered character	✗	Typographic design
Invert	↺	Typographic design
Close-up	⌒	Typo graphic design
Add space	⌣	Typographic design
Subtract space	⌉	Typographic design
Transpose	∿	design Typographic
Take over	⌐	Typographic design Typo
Take back	⌐	graphic design
Run on	⌐	Typographic design is a skilled art.

put up   instruction on proof to change lower case to caps *(SEE* PROOF CORRECTION MARKS)

pvt   abbreviation for *page view terminal*

quad   in metal typesetting a piece of metal which being less than the type height does not take or transfer ink and therefore has no other function than to fill out lines of type where large white spaces are required;

quad spaces are usually em quads, or en quads but may also be added in other multiples depending on the machine in use

(TYPE MARK-UP/EN/*SEE* QUADDING)

quadding   the addition of unusually large white spaces between words to fill out lines of type, eg *quad left*, *quad right*, *quad centre*

(TYPE MARK-UP/QUAD/*SEE* WORDSPACE)

quad left/right/centre   (*SEE* RANGE)

question mark ?   used after a sentence to indicate a direct question but not after an indirect question, or a sentence which includes its own answer; placed outside quotation marks

(FOUNT/SEMI COLON/*SEE* EXCLAMATION MARK)

quotation marks   single (' ') or double ('' '') are used to indicate direct quotes where distinction is not made by either a change of typesize or indentation of quoted matter;

single quotes are normally used and where a quote appears within a quote, then double quotes appear;

also known as inverted commas

(FOUNT/PIECE FRACTION/*SEE* SCRATCH COMMA)

radix the basis of any number system by positional notation
(NUMBER SYSTEMS/POSITIONAL NOTATION/*SEE* DECIMAL NOTATION)

ragged bodytext in which each line is to a different measure; consequently one side of the column will not line up horizontally;
also known as unjustified setting
(LAYOUT/HYPHENLESS JUSTIFICATION/*SEE* RANGE)

raised capital *upper case* character projecting above the line of type in which it is set and ranged along the baseline

We must learn that not everything in life can be bought and sold —

ram abbreviation for *random access memory*

random access memory (ram) (*SEE* CYCLIC STORE)

range in bodytext where each line is to a different measure, that edge of the column which lines up vertically, ie range left/ragged right, or range right/ragged left;
also known as flush left, right or quad left/quad right (LAYOUT/RAGGED/*SEE* CENTRE)

ranging figures (*SEE* LINING FIGURES)

raster   a line screen imposed over an image, eg half-tone process and *cathode ray tube*

raw tape   (*SEE* UNJUSTIFIED TAPE)

RC paper   abbreviation for *resin coated paper*

reading head   (*SEE* READ/WRITE HEAD)

read only memory (rom)   a memory store which holds permanent data only, and is not capable of being altered by program instructions
(SOFTWARE/MNEUMONIC CODING/*SEE* REMOTE ACCESS)

read/write head   an electromagnet used to read or write coded information on a magnetic store; magnetic disks and drums may have more than one read/write head thereby allowing *random access memory*
(HARDWARE/MAGNETIC DRUM/*SEE* COMPUTER)

real time   any computerised system in which the *input* generates an *output* of one form or another and virtually simultaneously
(SOFTWARE/REMOTE ACCESS/*SEE* OCR)

reference marks   special marks which relate footnotes to specific points in the main body of the text above; they usually appear in a consistent order
(FOUNT/ELLIPSES/*SEE* ASTERISK)

registered mark ®   mark denoting that a design has been registered as protection against plagiarism
(COPYRIGHT MARK /*SEE* FOUNT)

regular   the standard design of a typeface from which all other variations to weight and width are taken
(*SEE* TYPEFACE WEIGHT)

relative units   in machine composition all characters have a *set width* calculated in relative units; these increments are not standard like *points* but relate to the typesize in question; the unit is calculated by dividing the typesize *em* into vertical bands; for example on an 18 unit

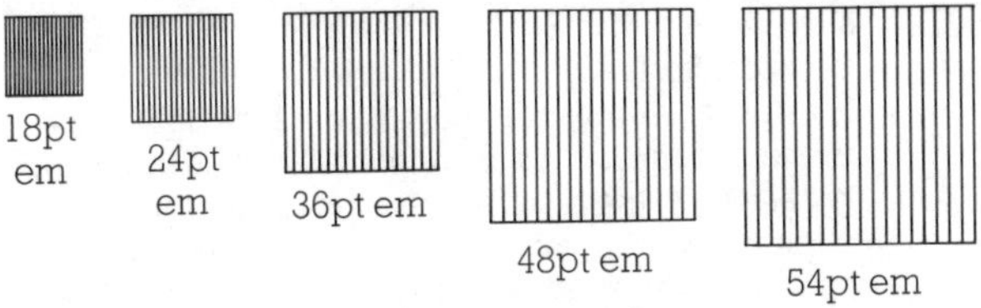

18pt
em

24pt
em

36pt em

48pt em

54pt em

Division of the em into 18 relative units

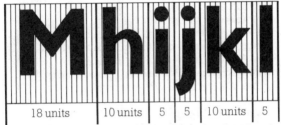

| 18 units | 10 units | 5 | 5 | 10 units | 5 |

Above: 72pt type showing the relative set widths of characters

Below: The relative set widths of various characters

|a|b|c|d|e|f|g|h|i|j|k|l|m|n|o|p|q|r|

|.|,|:|;|!|?|'|'|-|(|)|%|

|A|B|C|D|E|F|G|H|I|J|K|L|M|N|O|

|1|2|3|4|5|6|7|8|9|0|£|$|*|§|/|·

|⅓|⅔|⅛|¼|⅜|½|⅝|¾|⅞|©|@|

|á|à|â|ä|é|è|ê|ë|í|ì|î|ï|ó|ò|ô|ö|ú|ù|

system, and for 18pt type, each unit would then
be equal to 1pt;
for 9pt type each unit would then be equal to $\frac{1}{2}$pt;
therefore the unit is calculated by dividing the
typesize by the number of units to the em;
each typesetting system also has its own
specification of units to the em, eg the Quadritek
1200 works on 36 relative units to the em, the
Monotype Lasercomp has 96 relative units to the
em, and so on (SEE MEASURING SYSTEMS)

remote access   the ability to access a computer from
a keyboard terminal located at a distant location
from all other items of hardware
(SOFTWARE/READ ONLY MEMORY/SEE REAL TIME)

resin coated paper (RC paper)   photographic
material having a light sensitive paper base,
sandwiched between polyethylene layers (also
known as PE paper). To resolve the image this
material is wet-processed in a chemical solution
(HARDWARE/REVERSE-READING/SEE STABILISATION PAPER)

resolution   (SEE OUTPUT RESOLUTION)

resolve   the means by which computerised
photocomposition systems realise the characters
stored in an image master (SEE CHARACTER PROJECTION)

retrieval   the extraction of data from a magnetic store
of filed records (SOFTWARE/FILE/SEE KEYWORD INDEX)

reversal film   a type of photographic film in which
the black and white areas correspond to the
original but which may be made with the need of
an intermediary negative
(POSITIVE/SEE OUTPUT MATERIAL)

reverse field vdu   a visual display unit which
displays data as dark characters on a light
background
(HARDWARE/VISUAL DISPLAY UNIT/SEE MARCHING DISPLAY UNIT)

reverse indent   converse of indent, where all lines of

a paragraph except the first one are indented;
also known as hanging indent, as used here
(*SEE* HANGING PUNCTUATION)

reverse leading   (*SEE* REVERSE LINE-FEED)

reverse line feed   the ability of some
photocomposition machines to turn the
paper/film backwards and space type or blocks
of text within a defined area;
also referred to, less satisfactorily, as reverse
leading and reverse line spacing
(WHITE LINE/*SEE* TYPE MARK-UP)

reverse line spacing   (*SEE* REVERSE LINE FEED)

reverse reading   text set in a mirror image of its
original or final form and reading from
right to left;
may also be referred to as wrong reading
(HARDWARE/RIGHT READING/*SEE* RESIN COATED PAPER)

revise   US term synonymous for *revised proof*

revised proof   additional proof to show that original
corrections have been made satisfactorily
(PROOF CORRECTION MARKS/MASTER PROOF/*SEE* PAGE PROOFS)

right reading   text read in the normal manner from
left to right (HARDWARE/POSITIVE/*SEE* REVERSE READING)

rom   1) abbreviation for *read only memory*
2) abbreviation for *roman*

roman (rom)   in general all typefaces that stand
upright but, more specifically, those typefaces
having derived from *humanist* manuscripts
(CLASSIFICATION OF TYPE/*SEE* ITALIC)

roman numerals   seldom used system (except for
chapter headings) of marking numbers by the
use of capital letters
(CLASSIFICATION OF TYPE/ALPHANUMERIC/*SEE* ARABIC NUMERALS)

rough proof   synonymous for *galley proof*

run-around   layout of type in which individual lines
are calculated separately to fit around the usually

Fine typography is the result of nothing more than an attitude. Its appeal comes from the typographic understanding used in its planning; the designer must always care. This could mean using tight spacing, minus leading and different sizes and weights. In contemporary advertising, the perfect integration of design elements may possibly demand typography that is unorthodox.

irregular contour of an illustration or other display matter (LAYOUT /*SEE* BODYTEXT)

running text bodytext set to a standard specification but of such a length that the column depth must be broken to run over a number of columns or pages (LAYOUT /COLUMN DEPTH /*SEE* TYPE MARK-UP)

run on instruction on typescript or proof to signify that no new line or paragraph is required (*SEE* PROOF CORRECTION MARKS)

run-round (*SEE* RUN-AROUND)

S

sans serif generic term used to classify a wide range
of typefaces as those which are devoid of
finishing strokes on *stems* and other elements
(CLASSIFICATION OF TYPEFACES/TRANSITIONAL/*SEE* GEOMETRICAL
SANS SERIF)

ABCDEFGHIJKLMNOPQRS
TUVWXYZabcdefghijklmnop
qrstuvwxyz
ABCDEFGHIJKLMNOPQRSTU
VWXYZabcdefghijklmnopqr
stuvwxyz
ABCDEFGHIJKLMNOPQRSTUVW
XYZabcdefghijklmnopqrstuvwxyz
ABCDEFGHIJKLMNOPQR
STUVWXYZabcdefghijklmn
opqrstuvwxyz

sc abbreviation for *small capitals*
scanning in digitised characters the process by
which the character generator, whether an

electron or a laser beam, moves in sweeps
across a light sensitive base and is turned on and
off by the computer to re-create the original
character image back from its coded numerical
form in the matrix store;
because scanning beams can sweep in very fine
increments it is possible to program computers
to vary the information held in the matrix store to
automatically vary the weight/width and slant of a
single fount in an endless variety of permutations
(DIGITISATION/MATRIX STORE/*SEE* SOFTWARE)

scratch comma/ quotation mark in the form of a
solidus (FOUNT/QUOTATION MARKS/*SEE* FULL POINT)

script typefaces resembling handwriting and often

having evolved from chancery italic
(CLASSIFICATION OF TYPE/CHANCERY ITALIC/SEE BLACK LETTER)

ABCDEFGHIJKLMNOPQR STUVWXYZabcdefghijklmnopqrs tuvwxyz 1234567890(?)& .,;:!%

scrolling facility   the ability of a crt visual display
unit to rotate lines of text displayed on the screen
in a vertical direction;
this permits the operator to view a lengthy text
which might otherwise be outside the limited
display area of the screen
(HARDWARE/CATHODE RAY TUBE/SEE PAGE MAKE UP TERMINAL)

section §   fourth order reference mark
(FOUNT/DOUBLE DAGGER/SEE PARALLEL)

segmented disc   in photocomposition systems based
on the principle of character projection, an
image master in the form of quarter of a film disc;
each segment contains 1 font so that any four fonts
may be combined at the same time
(FILM STRIP/FILM DISC/SEE IMAGE MASTER)

semi colon ;   used to indicate a pause more marked
than a comma and less than a colon or full point;
used to separate items in a list having internal
punctuation;
usually appears outside quotation marks
(FOUNT/COLON/SEE QUESTION MARK)

serial interface   a device which allows characters to
be transmitted one after another between two
items of hardware and over long distances
(SEE PARALLEL INTERFACE)

serial store   here data is recorded as individual
characters along a length of tape in linear

sequence;
information can only be retrieved by sorting the data into sequence so that each may be examined in turn (HARDWARE/DATA CARRIER/*SEE* PAPER TAPE)

serif 1) short stroke at the ends of stems, arms and tails of characters (CHARACTER/SPINE/*SEE* BEAK)
2) serifs – generic term used to distinguish a wide range of otherwise dissimilar styles
(CLASSIFICATION OF TYPEFACES/*SEE* VENETIANS AND OLD FACES)

ABCDEFGHIJKLMNOPQ
RSTUVWXYZabcdefghijkl
mnopqrstuvwxyz

ABCDEFGHIJKLMNOPQR
STUVWXYZabcdefghijklm
nopqrstuvwxyz

ABCDEFGHIJKLMNOPQRST
UVWXYZabcdefghijklmnopqrst
uvwxyz

set contraction for *set width*
set solid an expression referring to lines of type set without any additional interline spacing
(TYPE MARK-UP/INTERLINE SPACING/*SEE* NEGATIVE INTERLINE SPACING)

set width   the fixed width of pieces of type calculated
according to the *unit system* of measurement
(TYPESIZE/*SEE* MEASURING TYPE)

shaded letters   synonymous with *shadow*
shadow   a group of inline/outline typefaces having a
shadow effect
(CLASSIFICATION OF TYPE/INLINE/*SEE* COMPOSITION SIZE)

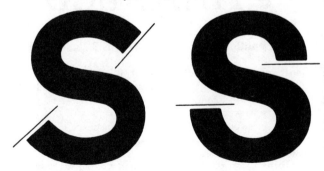

shear   the angle at which the terminal of a *character
stroke* is cleanly cut off (CHARACTER/*SEE* STROKE WIDTH)

shilling mark /   (*SEE* SOLIDUS)
slab serif   a group of typefaces having noticeably

square ended serifs;
most 19th century versions of these faces have
bracketed serifs, eg Clarendon whereas
20th century versions do not, eg Rockwell;
also known as square serifs

(GROTESQUE SANS SERIF /*SEE* CLASSIFICATION OF TYPEFACES)

slant/slash   (*SEE* SOLIDUS)
small capitals (sc)   capital letters drawn to the same
size as the lower case x-height of the alphabet in
use (FOUNT /LOWER CASE /*SEE* SUPERIOR CHARACTERS)

ghijk ABCDE

small caps   a contraction for *small capitals*
small fraction   one composed of small numerals,
eg $\frac{3}{4}$ (*SEE* CASE FRACTIONS)
software   a term used to identify all of those
procedures or operating instructions which help
the user to make best use of the hardware

1) (PHOTOCOMPOSITION /HARDWARE /*SEE* KEYBOARD)

2) (PHOTOCOMPOSITION /SOFTWARE /*SEE* LANGUAGE)

solid   (*SEE* SET SOLID)
solid fraction   (*SEE* CASE FRACTION)
solidus /   an oblique stroke which when used between
words indicates that the reader may choose
between them or that the following text is

a direct quote;
also used to indicate ratios, fractions, and in tabular material;
alternatively referenced to as *slash, oblique stroke, slant, shilling mark* and *scratch comma*
(FOUNT/BRACKETS/*SEE* BRACE)

sorts (*SEE* PI CHARACTERS)

spacing the separation of letters/words and lines of type by the addition of white space
(TYPE MARK-UP/*SEE* M)

spec abbreviation for *specification*

special sorts (*SEE* PI CHARACTERS)

specification synonymous in type design for *type mark-up*

spine the main stroke of the character s, minus the arms (CHARACTER/ARM/*SEE* SERIFS)

split fraction (*SEE* PIECE FRACTION)

spur the short spike at the base of the *stem* of the upper case G (CHARACTER/SWASH/*SEE* POTHOOK)

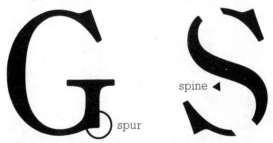

spine ◀

spur

square serif synonymous for *slab serif*

stabilisation paper a photographic material sensitive to ultra violet light and therefore to *resolve* the *character assembly* the material is dry-processed;
stabilisation paper has a lifespan of about six

weeks and for longer periods it must be fixed and washed

(HARDWARE/RESIN COATED PAPER/*SEE* DEFINITION)

stand alone   in some systems the computer is physically incorporated with the keyboard but where these items are separated they are referred to as a stand alone system

(HARDWARE/COMPUTER/*SEE* ON-LINE)

stem   all straight, vertical or near vertical, full length strokes of characters

(CHARACTER/STROKE WIDTH/*SEE* CROSS STROKE)

stet   instruction on proof to leave a correction in its original form and derived from the Latin 'let it stand' (*SEE* PROOF CORRECTION MARKS)

storage   the act of injecting data or programs into the *magnetic store* of a computer so that the data may be retained over a period of time

(SOFTWARE/K/*SEE* FILE)

stroke   contraction for either *character stroke* or *letterstroke*

stroke width   the relative width of mostly horizontal and vertical character strokes;
those typefaces having an apparently even stroke width are called *monoline*;
the variable stroke widths of some letters are called thicks and thins (CHARACTER/SHEAR/*SEE* STEM)

style   the look or 'feel' of a typeface (*SEE* STYLUS)

stylus   the pointed rod used by Greeks and Romans to write on tablets of wax;
because such tools influence the look of the letters that they produce, hence the origin of the term typestyle (CLASSIFICATION OF TYPE/*SEE* CUNIEFORM)

stylus printer   synonymous with *matrix printer*

superior characters   small characters set to appear near the capital height of a typesize, eg $A^2 B^3$

(FOUNT/SMALL CAPITALS/*SEE* INFERIOR CHARACTERS)

swash   an ornamental flourish added to some *upper case* characters;
may also be known as finial letter
(CHARACTER/FOOT/*SEE* SPUR)

ABDEFGH

T

tabbing   the arrangement of tabular material over a number of narrow columns;
computerised photocomposition systems usually incorporate a varying number of tab positions to facilitate this operation (*SEE* KEYBOARD)

tablet   contraction for digitising pad

tab position   (*SEE* TABBING)

tabular facility   the ability to set columns of type at pre-determined locations along a pica measure;
some machines have special tab positions available to the operator although the number of positions may vary from 5–100 and these are identified in the tables for photocomposition systems, Part III of this book (*SEE* TABBING)

tail   the stroke of a character which descends from left to right such as K, R, Q (CHARACTER/BAR/*SEE* ARM)

take back   instruction on proof to take words or lines of text back to the previous line, column or page
(*SEE* PROOF CORRECTION MARKS)

take in   instruction on proof to include additional copy (*SEE* PROOF CORRECTION MARKS)

take over   instruction on proof to remove words to

the following line of text or remove lines of text
to the subsequent column or page
(*SEE* PROOF CORRECTION MARKS)

tape (*SEE* PAPER TAPE/MAGNETIC TAPE)

tape merging (*SEE* MERGING)

tape reader a device which can decode the data
stored on a paper/magnetic tape, disk or drum
(*SEE* READ/WRITE HEAD)

Teletypesetter (TTS) the brand name for a system
where functions are controlled by a 6 level tape,
prepared on a perforator (*SEE* HARDWARE)

test program (*SEE* TRACE PROGRAM)

text types 1) in US synonymous for black letter
(OLD ENGLISH/*SEE* GOTHIC)

2) in UK synonymous for *composition size*

thicks and thins the variable stroke widths of
characters having evolved from the directional
movement of a pen in *calligraphy*
(CHARACTER/STROKE WIDTH/*SEE* STEM)

TQTQTQ

thins (*SEE* THICKS AND THINS)

thorn þ used in Anglo-Saxon and Icelandic to
represent the voiceless sound 'th' as in think
(DIACRITICAL MARKS/HACEK/*SEE* TILDE)

tied letter (*SEE* LIGATURE)

tilde ñ (DIACRITICAL MARKS/THORN/*SEE* UMLAUT)

top alignment the ability of some photocomposing
systems to align characters along the *capital line*
(*SEE* CENTRE ALIGNMENT)

TOP ALIGNING

trace parameters   a diagnostic set of variable quantities given fixed values to check for errors in either a formula or machine (in this book trace parameters have been included with the copyfitting programs so that the user may check the compatibility of his calculator to the formulae, presented as a sequence of keystrokes); should the data not tally then minor amendments to the specified keystrokes may have to be made
(SOFTWARE/PARAMETERS/*SEE* DATA)

trace program   a diagnostic program used to check and locate errors in either a machine or formula; may also be known as test program
(SOFTWARE/FLOWCHART/*SEE* PARAMETERS)

transitional   a group of serif typefaces dating from the mid 18th century and falling midway in development between venetians, old faces and the moderns; typeface examples are Fournier, Baskerville
(CLASSIFICATION OF TYPEFACES/MODERNS/*SEE* GEOMETRICAL SANS SERIF)

abcdefghij

ABCDEF

abcdefghijklm

ABCDEFG

transpose (trs)   instruction on proof to reverse the
   order of characters, words or lines of text
   (*SEE* PROOF CORRECTION MARKS)
trs   abbreviation for *transpose*
   (*SEE* PROOF CORRECTION MARKS)
TTS   abbreviation for *Teletypesetter*
type   the letters of the alphabet and all other
   characters used to create words, sentences and
   blocks of text (*SEE* CLASSIFICATION OF TYPEFACES)
typeface and typesize mix within a line   all
   photocomposition systems can mix different
   point sizes within a line, but the ability to combine
   this operation with a change of style or faces
   varies from system to system
   (*SEE* TYPEFACE MIX WITHIN A LINE)

mix mix **mix** mix

typeface mix within a line   a term used in the tables
   for photocomposition systems, Part III of this book,
   to identify the ability of different typesetting
   systems to set a variety of different typestyles or
   faces within a single line of setting;
   where this is possible the operation may have to
   be executed manually by the keyboard operator,
   and therefore be more expensive, or the setting
   system may hold a number of fount masters and
   perform the operation automatically;
   in this latter case the number and variety of
   permutations may be deduced by referring to
   founts per master and *image masters in machine*

mix mix

typeface weight   variations of blackness to the
       regular design of a typeface;
       there are no absolute standards for this type of
       classification, but a loose definition is extra light,
       light, semi light, regular, semi bold, bold, extra
       bold, ultra bold
       (CLASSIFICATION OF TYPE/TYPEFACE WIDTH/*SEE* FAMILY OF TYPE)
typeface width   variations to the width of a typeface
       have no standard classification but may be
       loosely termed ultra condensed, extra
       condensed, condensed, semi condensed,
       regular, semi expanded, expanded, extra
       expanded, ultra expanded
       (CLASSIFICATION OF TYPE/HEADLINE TYPE/*SEE* TYPEFACE WEIGHT)

ne

ne ne ne ne

ne ne ne ne

ne ne ne ne

ne ne ne

ne

typefactor in this publication, a number used to represent the relative *set width* of a named typeface and consequently to be used as an aid for computing complex copyfitting problems;

to calculate a typefactor – from a lower case alphabet or specimen of set text for a chosen typeface – see instructions provided at the beginning of Part V;

the typefactors in *Browns Index* are for use on English-language setting, being based on the incidence of characters as they appear in normal English text, including frequency of capital letters;

many such typefactors are listed in Part V, but it should be noted that they represent typefaces set with normal letter/word spacing;

if normal letter/word spacing is varied, either by adding or subtracting units, then the typefactor must also be modified accordingly;

instructions for calculating a *modified typefactor* for plus or minus letter/word spacing are given at the beginning of Part V;

where such modification to the typefactor is not made or accounted for, then significant variations in the copyfitting program will occur

type family synonymous for *family of type*

type mark-up instructions for the typesetter and made on the original typescript by the designer
(*SEE* LAYOUT/PROOF CORRECTION MARKS/SPACING)

typemaster (*SEE* IMAGE MASTER)

typescript the original copy before photocomposing and usually typed on either an *elite* or a *pica* *typewriter*

type series synonymous for *family of type*

typesetting the assembly of *characters* in a form suitable for reproduction by a printing medium

such as lithography;
in photocomposition techniques where two
distinct forms of typesetting are employed,
a more appropriate term to cover both is
character assembly

typesize   the measurement of any given typeface in
points and also referred to as the point size;
measurement is calculated from two lines of type,
without interline spacing, and calculated from
baseline to baseline
(MEASURING TYPE/X-HEIGHT/*SEE* SET WIDTH)

The breeding habitat
^
24pt **rocky coast with offsh**
v
and islands, with som

type style   the look or 'feel' of a typeface (*SEE* STYLUS)
typewriter faces   there are two standard sizes of
typewriter faces of which 'elite' will always have
12 characters to the inch and pica have 10
characters to the inch (*SEE* CHARACTER COUNT)

elite

```
We would like to call the meeting
grateful if you could indicate two
might be available to come down fo
```

pica

```
These notes refer to the rev
June 1983.  According to the
all full-time staff should r
```

uc   abbreviation for *upper case*

u/lc also u&lc   abbreviation for *upper and lower case*

umlaut ü   used to alter the sounds of a o u
(DIACRITICAL MARKS / TILDE / *SEE* BREVE)

unbracketed serif   serifs joined to the main stem of the character at a 90° angle (*SEE* BRACKETED SERIF)

unitisation   the practice of giving to machine set characters a specified width relative to their design, and calculated in relative units (not to be confused with digitisation) (*SEE* RELATIVE UNITS)

units to the em   a term used in the tables for photocomposition systems, Part III of this book, to identify the size of a relative unit in calculations of plus and minus letterspacing (*SEE* RELATIVE UNITS)

unit system   in the mechanical composition of type a method for calculating and relating the proportional widths of characters
(MEASURING SYSTEMS / INCREMENTS / *SEE* RELATIVE UNITS)

$€£†§.,:;!?'-

unit value   the fixed width of a piece of type
  (*SEE* SET WIDTH)
unit width   the fixed width of a piece of type
  (*SEE* SET WIDTH)
unjustified setting   (*SEE* RAGGED)
unjustified tape   tape output of a *non-counting
  keyboard*;
    here the operator makes no end of line decisions
    concerning *hyphenation and justification* and the
    computer must perform this task before the
    characters can be assembled in the photo unit;
    also known variously as raw tape, idiot tape, line-
    endless tape and endless tape
  (SOFTWARE/EXCEPTION DICTIONARY /*SEE* DIGITISATION)
upper case (uc)   all the capital letters of a fount;
    also known as majuscules
  (FOUNT /CHARACTER /*SEE* LOWER CASE)

usts   abbreviation for unified small *typesetting*
  system

van dyke (*SEE* OZALID PROOF)

vapour diazo (*SEE* OZALID PROOF)

vdt abbreviation for *visual display terminal*

vdu abbreviation for *visual display unit*

venetians and old faces two groups of serif
typefaces developed around the early 16th

abcdefghijkl

ABCDEFG

abcdefghijklm

ABCDEFGHI

abcdefghijklm

ABCDEFGHI

century and showing their calligraphic origins in
the lower case characters;
the stress is diagonal and the serifs are
bracketed and, except at the ends of descenders,
are given a consistent slant;
capitals are often shorter than the
ascender height;
venetian faces originally preceded the true old
faces retain the sloping bar to the '*e*' and only
slight variation to the thicks and thins;
examples of *venetians* are Centaur and Italian Old
Style, and for *old face* Bembo, Poliphilus, Blado,
Garamond, Plantin, Ehrhardt, Van Dijck, Caslon
(CLASSIFICATION OF TYPEFACES /SANS SERIF /*SEE* MODERNS)

vertical rules   a term used in the tables for
photocomposition systems, Part III of this book, to
identify whether or not different photocomposition
systems can automatically set vertical rules within
text areas

vet   abbreviation for *visual editing terminal*

visual display terminal (vdt)   synonymous with, but
not so accurate for, *visual editing terminal*

visual display unit (vdu)   illuminated screen
displaying data entered through a *keyboard*;
such units may be one *peripheral* in a visual
editing terminal *on-line* to a computer or may be
used as *stand alone* information terminals;
in many vdu's data is presented as white or
coloured characters on a black background
(HARDWARE /VISUAL EDITING TERMINAL /*SEE* REVERSE FIELD VDU)

visual editing terminal (vet)   a terminal at which
data entered through a keyboard, on-line to a
computer, is stored on tape and then presented
to the operator via a visual display unit for
amendments and revisions
(HARDWARE /COMPATIBILITY /*SEE* VISUAL DISPLAY UNIT)

weight *(SEE* TYPEFACE WEIGHT)

wf abbreviation for *wrong fount*
  (SEE PROOF CORRECTION MARKS)

white line an interline space equal to one line of the
  specified typesize
  (TYPE MARK-UP /NEGATIVE INTERLINE SPACING /*SEE* REVERSE
  LINE FEED)

white space *(SEE* SPACING)

width *(SEE* TYPEFACE WIDTH)

wire service data transmitted from a distant source
  and for use at a receiving terminal *(SEE* HARDWARE)

word space the addition of white spaces between
  words is variable but, on average, may be
  calculated as either one en or one third of the em
  (TYPE MARK-UP /QUADDING /*SEE* LETTERSPACING)

accustomed to. But this is not to say that because we
have got used to something demonstrably less legible

is accustomed to. But this is not to say that because
we have got used to something demonstrably less

one is accustomed to. But this is not to say that
because we have got used to something

writing to fit where a designer is required to
  calculate the number of words that must be
  written to make a given typeface, of a specified
  typesize and fixed interline spacing, fit within a
  pre-determined area;
  the opposite of *copyfitting*

wrong fount (wf) the accidental use of a character
  from a different typeface *(SEE* PROOF CORRECTION MARKS)

wrong reading synonymous with *reverse reading*

x-height   the mean height of lower case letters,
exclusive of ascenders and descenders, and
measured from baseline to mean line
(MEASURING TYPE/MEANLINE/*SEE* TYPESIZE)

VWXYZ

In 1784, 'The Marriage of Figaro' by Beaumarchais,
came out at Paris, where it was acted with astonishing
success. Thomas Holcroft no sooner received notice of
this piece, than he formed the instant resolution of going

In 1784, 'The Marriage of Figaro' by Beaumarchais, came out at Paris, where it was acted with
astonishing success. Thomas Holcroft no sooner
received notice of this piece, than he formed the

**In 1784, 'The Marriage of Figaro' by Beau-
marchais, came out at Paris, where it was
acted with astonishing success. Thomas
Holcroft no sooner received notice of this**

---

examples of type set solid at a single size and
demonstrating variations to the x height in
different founts.

x-line   synonymous for *mean line*

Part II Spacing

The samples of spacing on the following pages are not intended to be comprehensive but to give only an indication of the changes that occur to the readability and texture of type through the modification of horizontal and vertical spacing.

When specifying letter and word spacing it is sometimes easier to use the general terms; normal, tight, loose, very tight. This is more so when the user is not fully conversant with the unit system. All of the following samples are numbered from 1–36 and Table 1, opposite, is intended to assist in the identification of a particular variable. Under each of the headings are given three alternative numbers and reading from left to right they refer to samples with: 0 linespacing, 1 pt linespacing, 2 pt linespacing. For example sample number 11 will have normal letterspacing, loose word spacing and 1 pt linespacing.

All of the samples shown here have been set in a single typesize on a system that has 96 relative units to the em, and each sample shows the number of units by which spacing has been adjusted. If the user wishes to convert a selected sample to a different system but still maintain the chosen spacing then Table 2 will show the equivalent number of units required for that specification. For example 16 units in a 96/100 unit system will equal 8 units in a 48 unit system, and so on.

The user should also note the modification that takes place to a normal typefactor with + and − letter and wordspacing. The program for making this calculation may be found on page 226, from which it is possible to modify any of the standard typefactors provided in Part V to allow for other than normal letter and wordspacing. The standard typefactor for Monotype

Gill Sans regular used for the sample settings is 24.96 (page 256) and the resulting samples of this text face with normal letter and wordspacing are provided with the sample settings 10, 11 and 12 on page 125.

Table 1. Adjusted letter and wordspace sample settings on 0, 1pt and 2pt interline spacing

		WORDSPACING		
		tight	**normal**	**loose**
	very tight	31 32 33	28 29 30	34 35 36
	tight	16 17 18	7 8 9	22 23 24
	normal	4 5 6	1 2 3	10 11 12
	loose	25 26 27	13 14 15	19 20 21
		0 1 2	**0 1 2**	**0 1 2**
		LINESPACING		

(LETTERSPACING is labelled vertically on the left)

Table 2. Equivalents of units used for letter and wordspace adjustments in sample settings

Units to em	96/100	54	48	36	18
	32	18	16	12	6
	27	15	13/14	10	5
	16	9	8	6	3
	10	5/6	5	4	2
	5	3	2/3	2	1

1 *letterspacing* 0 units *wordspacing* 27 units *linespacing* 0 pt *typefactor* 26.81

'Legibility, in practice, amounts simply to what one
is accustomed to. But this is not to say that because
we have got used to something demonstrably less
legible than something else would be if we could
get used to it, we should make no effort to scrap
the existing thing. This was done by the Florentines
and Romans of the fifteenth century; it requires
simply good sense in the originators and good will
in the rest of us'.

2 *letterspacing* 0 units *wordspacing* 27 units *linespacing* 1 pt *typefactor* 26.81

'Legibility, in practice, amounts simply to what one
is accustomed to. But this is not to say that because
we have got used to something demonstrably less
legible than something else would be if we could
get used to it, we should make no effort to scrap
the existing thing. This was done by the Florentines
and Romans of the fifteenth century; it requires
simply good sense in the originators and good will
in the rest of us'.

3 *letterspacing* 0 units *wordspacing* 27 units *linespacing* 2 pt *typefactor* 26.81

'Legibility, in practice, amounts simply to what one
is accustomed to. But this is not to say that because
we have got used to something demonstrably less
legible than something else would be if we could
get used to it, we should make no effort to scrap
the existing thing. This was done by the Florentines
and Romans of the fifteenth century; it requires
simply good sense in the originators and good will
in the rest of us'.

4 *letterspacing* 0 units *wordspacing* 16 units *linespacing* 0 pt *typefactor* 28.01

'Legibility, in practice, amounts simply to what one is
accustomed to. But this is not to say that because we
have got used to something demonstrably less legible
than something else would be if we could get used to
it, we should make no effort to scrap the existing
thing. This was done by the Florentines and Romans
of the fifteenth century; it requires simply good sense
in the originators and good will in the rest of us'.

5 *letterspacing* 0 units *wordspacing* 16 units *linespacing* 1 pt *typefactor* 28.01

'Legibility, in practice, amounts simply to what one is
accustomed to. But this is not to say that because we
have got used to something demonstrably less legible
than something else would be if we could get used to
it, we should make no effort to scrap the existing
thing. This was done by the Florentines and Romans
of the fifteenth century; it requires simply good sense
in the originators and good will in the rest of us'.

6 *letterspacing* 0 units *wordspacing* 16 units *linespacing* 2 pt *typefactor* 28.01

'Legibility, in practice, amounts simply to what one is
accustomed to. But this is not to say that because we
have got used to something demonstrably less legible
than something else would be if we could get used to
it, we should make no effort to scrap the existing
thing. This was done by the Florentines and Romans
of the fifteenth century; it requires simply good sense
in the originators and good will in the rest of us'.

7 *letterspacing* −5 units *wordspacing* 27 units *linespacing* 0 pt *typefactor* 29.69

'Legibility, in practice, amounts simply to what one is accustomed to. But this is not to say that because we have got used to something demonstrably less legible than something else would be if we could get used to it, we should make no effort to scrap the existing thing. This was done by the Florentines and Romans of the fifteenth century; it requires simply good sense in the originators and good will in the rest of us'.

8 *letterspacing* −5 units *wordspacing* 27 units *linespacing* 1 pt *typefactor* 29.69

'Legibility, in practice, amounts simply to what one is accustomed to. But this is not to say that because we have got used to something demonstrably less legible than something else would be if we could get used to it, we should make no effort to scrap the existing thing. This was done by the Florentines and Romans of the fifteenth century; it requires simply good sense in the originators and good will in the rest of us'.

9 *letterspacing* −5 units *wordspacing* 27 units *linespacing* 2 pt *typefactor* 29.69

'Legibility, in practice, amounts simply to what one is accustomed to. But this is not to say that because we have got used to something demonstrably less legible than something else would be if we could get used to it, we should make no effort to scrap the existing thing. This was done by the Florentines and Romans of the fifteenth century; it requires simply good sense in the originators and good will in the rest of us'.

10 *letterspacing* 0 units *wordspacing* 32 units *linespacing* 0 pt *typefactor* 24.96

'Legibility, in practice, amounts simply to what
one is accustomed to. But this is not to say that
because we have got used to something
demonstrably less legible than something else
would be if we could get used to it, we should
make no effort to scrap the existing thing. This
was done by the Florentines and Romans of the
fifteenth century; it requires simply good sense in
the originators and good will in the rest of us'.

11 *letterspacing* 0 units *wordspacing* 32 units *linespacing* 1 pt *typefactor* 24.96

'Legibility, in practice, amounts simply to what
one is accustomed to. But this is not to say that
because we have got used to something
demonstrably less legible than something else
would be if we could get used to it, we should
make no effort to scrap the existing thing. This
was done by the Florentines and Romans of the
fifteenth century; it requires simply good sense in
the originators and good will in the rest of us'.

12 *letterspacing* 0 units *wordspacing* 32 units *linespacing* 2 pt *typefactor* 24.96

'Legibility, in practice, amounts simply to what
one is accustomed to. But this is not to say that
because we have got used to something
demonstrably less legible than something else
would be if we could get used to it, we should
make no effort to scrap the existing thing. This
was done by the Florentines and Romans of the
fifteenth century; it requires simply good sense in
the originators and good will in the rest of us'.

'Legibility, in practice, amounts simply to what
one is accustomed to. But this is not to say that
because we have got used to something
demonstrably less legible than something else
would be if we could get used to it, we should
make no effort to scrap the existing thing. This
was done by the Florentines and Romans of the
fifteenth century; it requires simply good
sense in the originators and good will in the

'Legibility, in practice, amounts simply to what
one is accustomed to. But this is not to say that
because we have got used to something
demonstrably less legible than something else
would be if we could get used to it, we should
make no effort to scrap the existing thing. This
was done by the Florentines and Romans of the
fifteenth century; it requires simply good
sense in the originators and good will in the

'Legibility, in practice, amounts simply to what
one is accustomed to. But this is not to say that
because we have got used to something
demonstrably less legible than something else
would be if we could get used to it, we should
make no effort to scrap the existing thing. This
was done by the Florentines and Romans of the
fifteenth century; it requires simply good
sense in the originators and good will in the

'Legibility, in practice, amounts simply to what one is
accustomed to. But this is not to say that because we have
got used to something demonstrably less legible than
something else would be if we could get used to it, we
should make no effort to scrap the existing thing. This was
done by the Florentines and Romans of the fifteenth
century; it requires simply good sense in the originators
and good will in the rest of us'.

'Legibility, in practice, amounts simply to what one is
accustomed to. But this is not to say that because we have
got used to something demonstrably less legible than
something else would be if we could get used to it, we
should make no effort to scrap the existing thing. This was
done by the Florentines and Romans of the fifteenth
century; it requires simply good sense in the originators
and good will in the rest of us'.

'Legibility, in practice, amounts simply to what one is
accustomed to. But this is not to say that because we have
got used to something demonstrably less legible than
something else would be if we could get used to it, we
should make no effort to scrap the existing thing. This was
done by the Florentines and Romans of the fifteenth
century; it requires simply good sense in the originators
and good will in the rest of us'.

19 *letterspacing* +5 units *wordspacing* 32 units *linespacing* 0 pt *typefactor* 24.02

'Legibility, in practice, amounts simply to
what one is accustomed to. But this is not to
say that because we have got used to
something demonstrably less legible than
something else would be if we could get used
to it, we should make no effort to scrap the
existing thing. This was done by the
Florentines and Romans of the fifteenth
century; it requires simply good sense in the

20 *letterspacing* +5 units *wordspacing* 32 units *linespacing* 1 pt *typefactor* 24.02

'Legibility, in practice, amounts simply to
what one is accustomed to. But this is not to
say that because we have got used to
something demonstrably less legible than
something else would be if we could get used
to it, we should make no effort to scrap the
existing thing. This was done by the
Florentines and Romans of the fifteenth
century; it requires simply good sense in the

21 *letterspacing* +5 units *wordspacing* 32 units *linespacing* 2 pt *typefactor* 24.02

'Legibility, in practice, amounts simply to
what one is accustomed to. But this is not to
say that because we have got used to
something demonstrably less legible than
something else would be if we could get used
to it, we should make no effort to scrap the
existing thing. This was done by the
Florentines and Romans of the fifteenth
century; it requires simply good sense in the

'Legibility, in practice, amounts simply to what one is accustomed to. But this is not to say that because we have got used to something demonstrably less legible than something else would be if we could get used to it, we should make no effort to scrap the existing thing. This was done by the Florentines and Romans of the fifteenth century; it requires simply good sense in the originators and good will in the rest of us'.

'Legibility, in practice, amounts simply to what one is accustomed to. But this is not to say that because we have got used to something demonstrably less legible than something else would be if we could get used to it, we should make no effort to scrap the existing thing. This was done by the Florentines and Romans of the fifteenth century; it requires simply good sense in the originators and good will in the rest of us'.

'Legibility, in practice, amounts simply to what one is accustomed to. But this is not to say that because we have got used to something demonstrably less legible than something else would be if we could get used to it, we should make no effort to scrap the existing thing. This was done by the Florentines and Romans of the fifteenth century; it requires simply good sense in the originators and good will in the rest of us'.

25 *letterspacing* +5 units *wordspacing* 16 units *linespacing* 0 pt *typefactor* 25.43

'Legibility, in practice, amounts simply to what one is accustomed to. But this is not to say that because we have got used to something demonstrably less legible than something else would be if we could get used to it, we should make no effort to scrap the existing thing. This was done by the Florentines and Romans of the fifteenth century; it requires simply good sense in the originators and good will in the rest of us'.

26 *letterspacing* +5 units *wordspacing* 16 units *linespacing* 1 pt *typefactor* 25.43

'Legibility, in practice, amounts simply to what one is accustomed to. But this is not to say that because we have got used to something demonstrably less legible than something else would be if we could get used to it, we should make no effort to scrap the existing thing. This was done by the Florentines and Romans of the fifteenth century; it requires simply good sense in the originators and good will in the rest of us'.

27 *letterspacing* +5 units *wordspacing* 16 units *linespacing* 2 pt *typefactor* 25.43

'Legibility, in practice, amounts simply to what one is accustomed to. But this is not to say that because we have got used to something demonstrably less legible than something else would be if we could get used to it, we should make no effort to scrap the existing thing. This was done by the Florentines and Romans of the fifteenth century; it requires simply good sense in the originators and good will in the rest of us'.

'Legibility, in practice, amounts simply to what one is accustomed to. But this is not to say that because we have got used to something demonstrably less legible than something else would be if we could get used to it, we should make no effort to scrap the existing thing. This was done by the Florentines and Romans of the fifteenth century; it requires simply good sense in the originators and good will in the rest of us'.

'Legibility, in practice, amounts simply to what one is accustomed to. But this is not to say that because we have got used to something demonstrably less legible than something else would be if we could get used to it, we should make no effort to scrap the existing thing. This was done by the Florentines and Romans of the fifteenth century; it requires simply good sense in the originators and good will in the rest of us'.

'Legibility, in practice, amounts simply to what one is accustomed to. But this is not to say that because we have got used to something demonstrably less legible than something else would be if we could get used to it, we should make no effort to scrap the existing thing. This was done by the Florentines and Romans of the fifteenth century; it requires simply good sense in the originators and good will in the rest of us'.

'Legibility, in practice, amounts simply to what one is accustomed to. But this is not to say that because we have got used to something demonstrably less legible than something else would be if we could get used to it, we should make no effort to scrap the existing thing. This was done by the Florentines and Romans of the fifteenth century; it requires simply good sense in the originators and good will in the rest of us'.

'Legibility, in practice, amounts simply to what one is accustomed to. But this is not to say that because we have got used to something demonstrably less legible than something else would be if we could get used to it, we should make no effort to scrap the existing thing. This was done by the Florentines and Romans of the fifteenth century; it requires simply good sense in the originators and good will in the rest of us'.

'Legibility, in practice, amounts simply to what one is accustomed to. But this is not to say that because we have got used to something demonstrably less legible than something else would be if we could get used to it, we should make no effort to scrap the existing thing. This was done by the Florentines and Romans of the fifteenth century; it requires simply good sense in the originators and good will in the rest of us'.

'Legibility, in practice, amounts simply to what one is
accustomed to. But this is not to say that because we have got
used to something demonstrably less legible than something
else would be if we could get used to it, we should make no
effort to scrap the existing thing. This was done by the
Florentines and Romans of the fifteenth century; it requires
simply good sense in the originators and good will in the rest
of us'.

'Legibility, in practice, amounts simply to what one is
accustomed to. But this is not to say that because we have got
used to something demonstrably less legible than something
else would be if we could get used to it, we should make no
effort to scrap the existing thing. This was done by the
Florentines and Romans of the fifteenth century; it requires
simply good sense in the originators and good will in the rest
of us'.

'Legibility, in practice, amounts simply to what one is
accustomed to. But this is not to say that because we have got
used to something demonstrably less legible than something
else would be if we could get used to it, we should make no
effort to scrap the existing thing. This was done by the
Florentines and Romans of the fifteenth century; it requires
simply good sense in the originators and good will in the rest
of us'.

Part III Systems

Alphatype	Alphasette	CRS/Multiset III
1 Typesizes		
Minimum typesize	5pt	5pt
Maximum typesize	18pt	48pt
Increment for typesize increase	Fixed sizes	0.5pt

2 Letter and interline spacing

Units to the em	18	18
Plus letterspacing: min/max	0.5–5 units	0.125–9.875 units
Minus letterspacing: min/max	0.5–5 units	0.125–9.875 units
Kerning facility	Yes	Yes (255 pairs)
Maximum interline spacing	39pt	999pt
Increment for interline spacing	0.25pt	0.125pt
Reverse line-feed	Optional	Yes

3 Mixing typefaces and sizes

Typeface mix within a line	Yes	Yes
Automatic typeface mix	Yes	Yes (31)
Typesize mix within a line	Yes	Yes
Automatic typesize mix	Yes	Yes (31)
Typeface/size mix within a line	Yes	Yes
Baseline alignment	Yes	Yes
Centre alignment	–	Manually
Top alignment	–	Manually

4 Output material

Maximum measure	66 pica ems	94 pica ems
Output on paper	Yes	Yes
Output on film	Yes	Yes
Paper/film widths	305–381mm	102–406mm

– = Not applicable to system/information not available

5 Hyphenation and tabbing

	Alphasette	CRS/Multiset III
Input	Paper, Magnetic tape	Paper, Mag tape/Floppy disk/OCR/Data phone
Unjustified tapes	Yes	Yes
Hyphenless justification	Yes	Yes
Discretionary justification	Yes	Yes
Logic justification	Optional	Yes
Exception dictionary justification	No	Yes (150 000 words)
Tabular facility	Yes	Yes
Number of tab positions	Optional	32
Tab: range left	Yes	Yes
Tab: range right	Yes	Yes
Tab: centred	Yes	Yes

6 Rules

Horizontal rules	–	Yes
Vertical rules	–	Yes
Box rules	–	Yes

7 Fount make-up

Image master	Film grid	Digital
Founts per master	2	Variable
Characters per typeface	84	232
Pi positions	Yes	Yes
Pi positions from stock	Yes	Yes

8 Fount storage and retrieval

Image masters in machine	5	1 000
Character capacity	840	7 192
Characters per second	10	40

— = Not applicable to system/information not available

Autologic	APS–5	APS Micro–5

1 Typesizes

Minimum typesize	5pt	5pt
Maximum typesize	192pt	192pt
Increment for typesize increase	0.1pt	0.1pt

2 Letter and interline spacing

Units to the em	100	100
Plus letterspacing: min/max	0.1pt–∞	0.1pt–∞
Minus letterspacing: min/max	0.1pt–∞	0.1pt–∞
Kerning facility	Yes	Yes
Maximum interline spacing	Paper/film limit	Paper/film limit
Increment for interline spacing	0.1pt	0.1pt
Reverse line-feed	Yes	Yes

3 Mixing typefaces and sizes

Typeface mix within a line	Yes	Yes
Automatic typeface mix	Yes	Yes
Typesize mix within a line	Yes	Yes
Automatic typesize mix	Yes	Yes
Typeface/size mix within a line	Yes	Yes
Baseline alignment	Yes	Yes
Centre alignment	Yes	Yes
Top alignment	Yes	Yes

4 Output material

Maximum measure	57/70/100 pica ems	45/57/70 pica ems
Output on paper	Yes	Yes
Output on film	Yes	Yes
Paper/film widths	0–423mm	0–423mm

5 Hyphenation and tabbing

	APS–5	APS Micro–5
Input	Paper, Magnetic tape/ Floppy cassette	Paper, Magnetic tape/ Floppy cassette
Unjustified tapes	Yes	Yes
Hyphenless justification	Optional	Optional
Discretionary justification	Optional	Optional
Logic justification	Yes	Yes
Exception dictionary justification	Yes	Yes
Tabular facility	Yes	Yes
Number of tab positions	Unlimited	Unlimited
Tab: range left	Yes	Yes
Tab: range right	Yes	Yes
Tab: centred	Yes	Yes

6 Rules

Horizontal rules	Yes	Yes
Vertical rules	Yes	Yes
Box rules	Yes	Yes

7 Fount make-up

Image master	Digital	Digital
Founts per master	1	1
Characters per typeface	128	128
Pi positions	Yes	Yes
Pi positions from stock	Yes	Yes

8 Fount storage and retrieval

Image masters in machine	Unlimited	Unlimited
Character capacity	Unlimited	Unlimited
Characters per second	5 000	5 000

Berthold

	Diatype	Vario/Diatext Standard	Diatronic DC3
1 Typesizes			
Minimum typesize	52pt	4ptD	6ptD
Maximum typesize	463pt	16ptD	20ptD
Increment for typesize increase	No standard	1ptD	1ptD

2 Letter and interline spacing

Units to the em	–	48	48
Plus letterspacing: min/max	0–6mm	–	1–11 units
Minus letterspacing: min/max	0–4mm	–	1–4 units
Kerning facility	Manually	Manually	Manually
Maximum interline spacing	35pt	9.75mm	15.94mm*
Increment for interline spacing	1pt	0.025mm	0.0625mm
Reverse line-feed	Yes	No	Yes

3 Mixing typefaces and sizes

Typeface mix within a line	Yes	Yes	Yes
Automatic typeface mix	No	Yes (2)†	Yes (8)
Typesize mix within a line	Yes	Yes	Yes
Automatic typesize mix	No	Yes (11)†	No
Typeface/size mix within a line	Manually	Yes†	Yes‡
Baseline alignment	Yes	Yes	Yes
Centre alignment	Manually	No	Yes
Top alignment	Manually	No	Yes

4 Output material

Maximum measure	48 pica ems	45 pica ems	71 pica ems
Output on paper	Yes	Yes	Yes
Output on film	Yes	Yes	Yes
Paper/film widths	297 × 210mm §	101–203mm	305 × 305mm §

– = Not applicable to system/information not available

* To 300mm manually   † Manually on Diatext Standard

Diatronic S	CPS 1000/ 1100/1200 1 Floppy 2 Floppy	CPS 2000/ 2100/2200 1 Floppy 2 Floppy	ACS 3200 2 Floppy
6ptD	5ptD	5ptD	5ptD
20ptD	36ptD	36ptD	36ptD
1ptD	0.01mm	0.01mm	0.01mm
48	48	48	48
1 – 11 units	1 unit – paper width	1 unit – paper width	1 unit – paper width
1 – 4 units	1 – 4 units	1 – 4 units	1 – 4 units
Manually	Yes	Yes	Yes
15.94mm*	300mm	300mm	300mm
0.0625mm	0.0625mm	0.0625mm	0.0625mm
Yes	Yes	Yes	Yes
Yes	Yes	Yes	Yes
Yes (8)	Yes (4)	Yes (8)	Yes (8)
Yes	Yes	Yes	Yes
Yes (all sizes)	Yes (all sizes)	Yes (all sizes)	Yes (all sizes)
Yes	Yes	Yes	Yes
Yes	Yes	Yes	Yes
Yes	Yes	Yes	Yes
Yes	Yes	Yes	Yes
71 pica ems	71 pica ems	71 pica ems	71 pica ems
Yes	Yes	Yes	Yes
Yes	Yes	Yes	Yes
305 × 305mm §	305 × 305mm §	305 × 305mm §	305 × 305mm §

‡ *With manual size change*　　　　　§ *paper/film supplied in sheets*

Berthold

	Diatype	Vario/ Diatext Standard	Diatronic DC3
5 Hyphenation and tabbing			
Input	–	Magnetic tape option	Direct entry
Unjustified tapes	No	No	–
Hyphenless justification	–	Yes	–
Discretionary justification	–	Yes	–
Logic justification	No	Yes	No
Exception dictionary justification	No	No	No
Tabular facility	Yes	Yes	Yes
Number of tab positions	6	6	300
Tab: range left	Yes	Yes	Yes
Tab: range right	No	Yes	Yes
Tab: centred	No	Yes	Yes
6 Rules			
Horizontal rules	Yes	Yes	Yes
Vertical rules	Yes	No	Yes
Box rules	Manually	No	Manually
7 Fount make-up			
Image master	Glass disc	Glass disc	Glass grid
Founts per master	1 or 2 (rom/ital)	2 (rom/ital)	2 (rom/ital)
Characters per typeface	196	126	126
Pi positions	No	No	Yes (pi grid)
Pi positions from stock	Yes	Yes/limited	Yes
8 Fount storage and retrieval			
Image masters in machine	1	1	8
Character capacity	196	252	1 008
Characters per second	Variable to operators skill	5	Variable to operators skill

– = Not applicable to system/information not available

Diatronic S	CPS 1000/1100/1200 1 Floppy 2 Floppy	CPS 2000/2100/2200 1 Floppy 2 Floppy	ACS 3200 2 Floppy
Paper, Magnetic tape	Floppy disk	Floppy disk	Floppy disk
No	No	No	No
–	Yes	Yes	Yes
–	Yes	Yes	Yes
–	Yes	Yes	Yes
–	Optional	Optional	Optional
Yes	Yes	Yes	Yes
300	16	16	16
Yes	Yes	Yes	Yes
Yes	Yes	Yes	Yes
Yes	Yes	Yes	Yes
Yes	Yes	Yes	Yes
Yes	Yes	Yes	Yes
Manually	Yes	Yes	Yes
Glass grid	Glass grid	Glass grid	Glass grid
1	1	1	1
126	126	126	126
Yes (pi grid)	Yes	Yes	Yes
Yes	Yes	Yes	Yes
8	4	8	8
1 008	504	1 008	1 008
10	11	11	11

— = Not applicable to system/information not available

Bobst–Graphic	Photoset 153–17	Photoset 133–8

1 Typesizes

Minimum typesize	5pt	5pt
Maximum typesize	48pt	36pt
Increment for typesize increase	Fixed sizes	Fixed sizes

2 Letter and interline spacing

Units to the em	18	18
Plus letterspacing: min/max	1 unit–∞	1 unit–∞
Minus letterspacing: min/max	1 – 99 units	1 – 99 units
Kerning facility	Yes	Yes
Maximum interline spacing	864pt	864pt
Increment for interline spacing	0.25pt	0.25pt
Reverse line-feed	Yes	Yes

3 Mixing typefaces and sizes

Typeface mix within a line	Yes	Yes)
Automatic typeface mix	Yes (8)	Yes (8)
Typesize mix within a line	Yes	Yes
Automatic typesize mix	Yes (17)	Yes (8)
Typeface/size mix within a line	Yes	Yes
Baseline alignment	Yes	Yes
Centre alignment	Manually	Manually
Top alignment	Manually	Manually

4 Output material

Maximum measure	69 pica ems	69 pica ems
Output on paper	Yes	Yes
Output on film	Yes	Yes
Paper/film widths	51 – 305mm	51 – 305mm

Photoset 143-8	Photoset 2001 CRT	Eurocat 120	Eurocat 150
5pt	6pt	5pt	5pt
36pt	96pt	36pt	36pt
Fixed sizes	0.1pt	Fixed sizes	Fixed sizes
18	100	36	36
1 unit-∞	1 - 100 units	1 unit-∞	1 unit-∞
1 - 99 units	*	1 - 99 units	1 - 99 units
Yes	*	No	Yes
864pt	Paper/film length	Paper/film length	Paper/film length
0.25pt	0.1pt	0.125pt	0.125pt
Yes	Yes	Yes	Yes
Yes	Yes	Yes	Yes
Yes (8)	Yes	-	-
Yes	Yes	-	-
Yes (8)	Yes	-	-
Yes	Yes	-	-
Yes	Yes	-	-
Manually	Manually	-	-
Manually	Manually	-	-
69 pica ems	70 pica ems	70 pica ems	70 pica ems
Yes	Yes	Yes	Yes
Yes	Yes	Yes	Yes
51 - 305mm	75 - 315mm	76 - 305mm	76 - 305mm

Dependent on front-end system installed

— = Not applicable to system/information not available

Bobst-Graphic	Photoset 153–17	Photoset 133–8
5 Hyphenation and tabbing		
Input	Floppy disk	Floppy disk
Unjustified tapes	Yes	Yes
Hyphenless justification	Optional	Optional
Discretionary justification	Optional	Optional
Logic justification	Optional	Optional
Exception dictionary justification	Yes (5 options)	Yes (5 options)
Tabular facility	Yes	Yes
Number of tab positions	31	31
Tab: range left	Yes	Yes
Tab: range right	Yes	Yes
Tab: centred	Yes	Yes
6 Rules		
Horizontal rules	Yes	Yes
Vertical rules	Yes	Yes
Box rules	Yes	Yes
7 Fount make-up		
Image master	Glass disc	Glass disc
Founts per master	8	8
Characters per typeface	126	126
Pi positions	Yes	Yes
Pi positions from stock	Yes	Yes
8 Fount storage and retrieval		
Image masters in machine	1	1
Character capacity	1 008	1 008
Characters per second	50	16

Photoset 143–8	Photoset 2001 CRT	Eurocat 120	Eurocat 150
Floppy disk	On-line to system	Cassette‡/ Floppy disk	Cassette‡/ Floppy disk
Yes	*	Optional	Optional
Optional	*	Optional	Optional
Optional	*	Optional	Optional
Optional	*	Optional	Optional
Yes (5 options)	*	Optional	Optional
Yes	Yes	Yes	Yes
31	*	31	31
Yes	Yes	Yes	Yes
Yes	Yes	Yes	Yes
Yes	Yes	Yes	Yes
Yes	Yes	Yes	Yes
Yes	Yes	Yes	Yes
Yes	Yes	Possible	Possible
Glass disc	Digital	Film strip/ Glass disc	Film strip/ Glass disc
8	4	8	8
126	160	126	126
Yes	Yes	Yes	Yes
Yes	Yes	Yes	Yes
1	200 +	1	1
1 008	32 000 +	1 008	1 008
32	556	–	–

Dependent on front-end system installed

‡ *With converter*   – = *Not applicable to system / information not available*

Compugraphic	Compuwriter I & II	ACM 9000

1 Typesizes

Minimum typesize	5pt	6pt
Maximum typesize	24pt	72pt
Increment for typesize increase	Fixed sizes	Fixed sizes

2 Letter and interline spacing

Units to the em	18	54
Plus letterspacing: min/max	1 unit–∞	1 unit–∞
Minus letterspacing: min/max	1–3 units	1–3 units
Kerning facility	No	No
Maximum interline spacing	31pt	99pt
Increment for interline spacing	0.5pt	0.5pt
Reverse line-feed	(I) No (II) Yes	Yes

3 Mixing typefaces and sizes

Typeface mix within a line	Yes	Yes
Automatic typeface mix	(I) No (II) Yes	Yes
Typesize mix within a line	Yes	Yes
Automatic typesize mix	Yes	Yes
Typeface/size mix within a line	Yes	Yes
Baseline alignment	Yes	Yes
Centre alignment	–	–
Top alignment	–	–

4 Output material

Maximum measure	45 pica ems	45 pica ems
Output on paper	Yes	Yes
Output on film	Yes	Yes
Paper/film widths	76–203mm	76–203mm

– = Not applicable to system/information not available

	2961 Series	4961 Series	Editwriter 7700	Editwriter 7500
	5pt	5pt	6pt	6pt
	24pt	24pt	72pt	72pt
	Fixed sizes	Fixed sizes	Fixed sizes	Fixed sizes
	18	18	54*	54*
	1 unit–∞	1 unit–∞	1 unit–∞	1 unit–∞
	1–3 units	1–3 units	1 unit–∞	1 unit–∞
	No	No	No	No
	31pt	31pt	99.5pt	99.5pt
	0.5pt	0.5pt	0.5pt	0.5pt
	No	No	Yes	Yes
	Yes	Yes	Yes	Yes
	Yes	Yes	Yes (8)	Yes (8)
	No	No	Yes	Yes
	No	No	Yes (12)	Yes (12)
	No	No	Yes	Yes
	Yes	Yes	Yes	Yes
	–	–	No	No
	–	–	No	No
	45 pica ems	45 pica ems	45 pica ems	45 pica ems
	Yes	Yes	Yes	Yes
	Yes	Yes	Yes	Yes
	76–203mm	76–203mm	51–203mm	51–203mm

Letterspacing in 18 units to em

– = Not applicable to system/information not available

Compugraphic	Compuwriter I & II	ACM 9000

5 Hyphenation and tabbing

Input	Direct input	Paper tape/Dir input
Unjustified tapes	No	Yes
Hyphenless justification	Yes	Yes
Discretionary justification	Yes	Yes
Logic justification	No	Yes
Exception dictionary justification	No	No
Tabular facility	Yes	Yes
Number of tab positions	9	9
Tab: range left	Yes	Yes
Tab: range right	Yes	Yes
Tab: centred	Yes	Yes

6 Rules

Horizontal rules	–	–
Vertical rules	–	–
Box rules	–	–

7 Fount make-up

Image master	Film strip	Film strip
Founts per master	(I) 2 (II) 4	4
Characters per typeface	96	102
Pi positions	No	No
Pi positions from stock	Yes	Yes

8 Fount storage and retrieval

Image masters in machine	1	2
Character capacity	192 – 384	816
Characters per second	–	12

– = *Not applicable to system/information not available*

	2961 Series	4961 Series	Editwriter 7700	Editwriter 7500
	Paper tape	Paper tape	Floppy disk	Floppy disk
	Yes	Yes	Yes	Yes
	Yes	Yes	Yes	Yes
	Yes	Yes	Yes	Yes
	Yes	Yes	Yes	Yes
	No	No	Optional	Optional
	Yes	Yes	Yes	Yes
	9	9	9 (3 modes)	9 (3 modes)
	Yes	Yes	Yes	Yes
	Yes	Yes	Yes	Yes
	Yes	Yes	Yes	Yes
	–	–	Yes	Yes
	–	–	Yes	Yes
	–	–	Yes	Yes
	Film strip	Film strip	Film strip	Film strip
	2	4	4	4
	96	96	128	128
	No	No	Yes	Yes
	Yes	Yes	Yes	Yes
	1	1	2	2
	192	384	1 024	1 024
	30	12	30	30

− = Not applicable to system/information not available

Compugraphic	Edit-writer 7900	Edit-writer 7770	8600

1 Typesizes

Minimum typesize	6pt	6pt	4pt
Maximum typesize	72pt	72pt	128pt
Increment for typesize increase	Fixed sizes	Fixed sizes	Fixed sizes

2 Letter and interline spacing

Units to the em	54*	54*	54
Plus letterspacing: min/max	1 unit–∞	1 unit–∞	1–99 units
Minus letterspacing: min/max	1 unit–∞	1 unit–∞	1–99 units
Kerning facility	No	No	No
Maximum interline spacing	99.5pt	99.5pt	1 736pt
Increment for interline spacing	0.5pt	0.5pt	0.125pt
Reverse line-feed	Yes	Yes	Yes

3 Mixing typefaces and sizes

Typeface mix within a line	Yes	Yes	Yes
Automatic typeface mix	Yes (8)	Yes (8)	Yes
Typesize mix within a line	Yes	Yes	Yes
Automatic typesize mix	Yes (12)	Yes (12)	Yes
Typeface/size mix within a line	Yes	Yes	Yes
Baseline alignment	Yes	Yes	Yes
Centre alignment	No	No	No
Top alignment	No	No	No

4 Output material

Maximum measure	45 pica ems	68 pica ems	45/68 pica ems
Output on paper	Yes	Yes	Yes
Output on film	Yes	Yes	Yes
Paper/film widths	51–203mm	51–305mm	203–305mm

Letterspacing to 18 units to em

	Edit-writer 7900	Edit-writer 7770	8600

5 Hyphenation and tabbing

Input	Floppy disk	Floppy disk	Paper tape/Mini disk/On-line
Unjustified tapes	Yes	Yes	Yes
Hyphenless justification	Yes	Yes	–
Discretionary justification	Yes	Yes	–
Logic justification	Yes	Yes	Yes
Exception dictionary	Optional	Optional	–
Tabular facility	Yes	Yes	Yes
Number of tab positions	9 (3 modes)	9 (3 modes)	99
Tab: range left	Yes	Yes	Yes
Tab: range right	Yes	Yes	Yes
Tab: centred	Yes	Yes	Yes

6 Rules

Horizontal rules	Yes	Yes	Yes
Vertical rules	Yes	Yes	Yes
Box rules	Yes	Yes	Yes

7 Fount make-up

Image master	Film strip	Film strip	Digital
Founts per master	4	4	1
Characters per typeface	128	128	80 – 254
Pi positions	Yes	Yes	Yes
Pi positions from stock	Yes	Yes	Yes

8 Fount storage and retrieval

Image masters in machine	2	2	100
Character capacity	1 024	1 024	25 400
Characters per second	30	30	500

— = Not applicable to system/information not available

1 Typesizes

Minimum typesize	4pt
Maximum typesize	96pt
Increment for typesize increase	4–12pt: 0.25pt 6–24pt: 0.5pt 12–48pt: 1pt 24–96pt: 2pt

2 Letter and interline spacing

Units to the em	–
Plus letterspacing: min/max	0.05pt–65 pica ems
Minus letterspacing: min/max	0.05pt–65 pica ems
Kerning facility	Yes
Maximum interline spacing	112pt
Increment for interline spacing	0.03125pt
Reverse line-feed	Yes

3 Mixing typefaces and sizes

Typeface mix within a line	Yes
Automatic typeface mix	Yes
Typesize mix within a line	Yes
Automatic typesize mix	Yes
Typeface/size mix within a line	Yes
Baseline alignment	Yes
Centre alignment	Yes
Top alignment	Yes

4 Output material

Maximum measure	70 pica ems
Output on paper	Yes
Output on film	Yes
Paper/film widths	76–305mm

– = Not applicable to system/information not available

5 Hyphenation and tabbing

Input	Paper, Magnetic tape/ Magnetic, Floppy disk/OCR
Unjustified tapes	Yes
Hyphenless justification	Yes
Discretionary justification	No
Logic justification	Yes
Exception dictionary justification	Yes
Tabular facility	Yes
Number of tab positions	30
Tab: range left	Yes
Tab: range right	Yes
Tab: centred	Yes

6 Rules

Horizontal rules	Yes
Vertical rules	Yes
Box rules	Yes

7 Fount make-up

Image master	Digital
Founts per master	1
Characters per typeface	138 – 250
Pi positions	Yes
Pi positions from stock	Yes

8 Fount storage and retrieval

Image masters in machine	1 600
Character capacity	80 mgbyte
Characters per second	350

Itek

	Quadritek 1200	1210/1211	Mark VIII
1 Typesizes			
Minimum typesize	5.5pt	5.5pt	5pt
Maximum typesize	36pt	72pt	72pt
Increment for typesize increase	5.5–12pt: 0.5pt 12–36pt: 1pt	5.5–12pt: 0.5pt 12–36pt: 1pt 36–72pt: 2pt	5–18pt: 0.5pt 18–72pt: 1pt
2 Letter and interline spacing			
Units to the em	36	36	108
Plus letterspacing: min/max	0.25– 99.25 units	0.25– 99.25 units	1 unit–∞
Minus letterspacing: min/max	1–99 units	1–99 units	1–99 units
Kerning facility	No	No	–
Maximum interline spacing	99.9pt	99.9pt	–
Increment for interline spacing	0.1pt	0.1pt	0.125pt
Reverse line-feed	Yes	Yes	Yes
3 Mixing typefaces and sizes			
Typeface mix within a line	Yes	Yes	Yes
Automatic typeface mix	Yes (4)	Yes (4)	Yes
Typesize mix within a line	Yes	Yes	Yes
Automatic typesize mix	Yes (57)	Yes (57)	Yes
Typeface/size mix within a line	Yes	Yes	Yes
Baseline alignment	Yes	Yes	Yes
Centre alignment	Yes	Yes	Yes
Top alignment	Manually	Manually	Yes
4 Output material			
Maximum measure	48 pica ems	48 pica ems	100 pica ems
Output on paper	Yes	Yes	Yes
Output on film	Yes	Yes	Yes
Paper/film widths	70–210mm	70–210mm	–

– = Not applicable to system / information not available

	Quadritek		
	1200	1210/1211	Mark VIII

5 Hyphenation and tabbing

Input	Floppy disk/ Mag tape	Floppy disk/ Mag tape	Flippy-floppy rigid disk
Unjustified tapes	No	No	Yes
Hyphenless justification	Yes	Yes	–
Discretionary justification	Yes	Yes	–
Logic justification	No	No	–
Exception dictionary	No	No	–
Tabular facility	Yes	Yes	Yes
Number of tab positions	20	20	–
Tab: range left	Yes	Yes	Yes
Tab: range right	Yes	Yes	Yes
Tab: centred	Yes	Yes	Yes

6 Rules

Horizontal rules	Yes	Yes	–
Vertical rules	Yes	Yes	–
Box rules	Yes	Yes	–

7 Fount make-up

Image master	Acrylic, seg- mented, disc	Acrylic, seg- mented, disc	Digital master
Founts per master	1	1	40
Characters per typeface	112	112	18pt master: 336 72pt master: 112
Pi positions	No	No	–
Pi positions from stock	Yes	Yes	–

8 Fount storage and retrieval

Image masters in machine	4	4	40
Character capacity	448	448	18pt master: 13 440 72pt master: 4 480
Characters per second	15	15	600

– = Not applicable to system/information not available

Mergenthaler Linotype Linoterm
Linoterm HS   Linotronic

1 Typesizes

Minimum typesize	6pt	4pt
Maximum typesize	36pt	48pt
Increment for typesize increase	Fixed sizes	Fixed sizes

2 Letter and interline spacing

Units to the em	18/54	54
Plus letterspacing: min/max	1 unit – paper width	1 unit – paper width
Minus letterspacing: min/max	1 – 99 units	1 – 99 units
Kerning facility	Yes (selective)	No
Maximum interline spacing	99.5pt	99.5pt
Increment for interline spacing	0.5pt	0.5pt
Reverse line-feed	Yes (to 0.5pt)	Yes

3 Mixing typefaces and sizes

Typeface mix within a line	Yes	Yes
Automatic typeface mix	Yes	Yes
Typesize mix within a line	Yes	Yes
Automatic typesize mix	Yes	Yes
Typeface/size mix within a line	Yes	Yes
Baseline alignment	Yes	Yes
Centre alignment	Yes	Yes
Top alignment	Yes	Yes

4 Output material

Maximum measure	45 pica ems	70 pica ems
Output on paper	Yes	Yes
Output on film	Yes	Yes
Paper/film widths	76 – 203mm	Sheets: 305 × 325mm

CRTronic	202N	404	606
4pt	4.5pt	4.5pt	4.5pt
36pt	72pt	96pt (caps to 160pt)	128pt (caps to 250pt)
–	0.5pt	0.5pt	0.5pt
54	54	54	54
1 unit – paper width	1 unit – ∞	1 unit – ∞	1 unit – ∞
1 – 99 units	1 – 99 units	1 – 99 units	1 – 99 units
No	–	–	–
–	–	–	–
–	0.25pt	0.25pt	0.0625pt
Yes	Yes	Yes	Yes
Yes	Yes	Yes	Yes
Yes	Yes	Yes	Yes
Yes	Yes	Yes	Yes
Yes	Yes	Yes	Yes
Yes	Yes	Yes	Yes
Yes	Yes	Yes	Yes
Yes	Yes	Yes	Yes
Yes	Yes	Yes	Yes
45 pica ems	48 pica ems	70 pica ems	100 pica ems
Yes	Yes	Yes	Yes
Yes	Yes	Yes	Yes
116 – 203mm	–	–	–

— = Not applicable to system/information not available

5 Hyphenation and tabbing

Input	Floppy disk/Paper tape	Floppy disk
Unjustified tapes	Yes	Yes
Hyphenless justification	Yes	–
Discretionary justification	Yes	–
Logic justification	Yes	–
Exception dictionary justification	No	–
Tabular facility	Yes	Yes
Number of tab positions	–	32
Tab: range left	Yes	Yes
Tab: range right	Yes	Yes
Tab: centred	Yes	Yes

6 Rules

Horizontal rules	Yes	Yes
Vertical rules	Yes	Yes
Box rules	Possible	Possible

7 Fount make-up

Image master	Film strip	Film strip
Founts per master	1	1
Characters per typeface	105	105
Pi positions	Yes	Yes
Pi positions from stock	Yes	Yes

8 Fount storage and retrieval

Image masters in machine	4	8
Character capacity	420	840
Characters per second	–	–

– = *Not applicable to system/information not available*

CRTronic	202N	404	606
Floppy disk	Floppy disk	Rigid disk	Rigid disk
Yes	Yes	Yes	Yes
–	–	–	–
–	–	–	–
–	–	–	–
–	–	–	–
Yes	Yes	Yes	Yes
32	–	–	–
Yes	Yes	Yes	Yes
Yes	Yes	Yes	Yes
Yes	Yes	Yes	Yes
Yes	–	–	–
No	–	–	–
–	–	–	–
Digital master	Digital master	Digital master	Digital master
1	1	5	5
125	121	121	121
No	–	–	–
No	–	–	–
1	2	1	1
–	7 260	13 310	159 720
–	450	3 000	3 000

– = Not applicable to system/information not available

Monotype			Lasercomp
	600	400	3000

1 Typesizes

Minimum typesize	6pt	5pt	5pt
Maximum typesize	28pt	24pt	256pt
Increment for typesize increase	–	–	0.25pt

2 Letter and interline spacing

Units to the em	18	18	96
Plus letterspacing: min/max	1 unit–∞	1 unit–∞	1–999 units
Minus letterspacing: min/max	1 unit–∞	1 unit–∞	1–999 units
Kerning facility	Yes	Yes	Yes
Maximum interline spacing	99pt	31pt	Paper/film length
Increment for interline spacing	0.5pt	0.5pt	0.25pt
Reverse line-feed	Yes	Yes	Yes

3 Mixing typefaces and sizes

Typeface mix within a line	Yes	Yes	Yes
Automatic typeface mix	Yes	No	Yes
Typesize mix within a line	Yes	Yes	Yes
Automatic typesize mix	Yes	No	Yes
Typeface/size mix within a line	Yes	Yes	Yes
Baseline alignment	Yes	Yes	Yes
Centre alignment	–	–	No
Top alignment	–	–	Yes

4 Output material

Maximum measure	52 pica ems	54 pica ems	58/100 pica ems
Output on paper	Yes	Yes	Yes
Output on film	Yes	Yes	Yes
Paper/film widths	153–254mm	153–254mm	150–430mm

– = Not applicable to system/information not available

	600	400	Lasercomp 3000

5 Hyphenation and tabbing

	600	400	Lasercomp 3000
Input	Paper, Mag tape	Paper tape	Paper, Mag tape/ Floppy disk
Unjustified tapes	No	No	Yes
Hyphenless justification	–	Yes	–
Discretionary justification	–	Yes	–
Logic justification	–	Yes	Yes
Exception dictionary	–	Optional	–
Tabular facility	Yes	Yes	Yes
Number of tab positions	20	20	20
Tab: range left	Yes	Yes	Yes
Tab: range right	Yes	Yes	Yes
Tab: centred	Yes	Yes	Yes

6 Rules

	600	400	Lasercomp 3000
Horizontal rules	–	–	Yes
Vertical rules	–	–	Yes
Box rules	–	–	Yes

7 Fount make-up

	600	400	Lasercomp 3000
Image master	Film disc	Film disc	Digital
Founts per master	Variable	Variable	Digital image for each size
Characters per typeface	Variable	Variable	128
Pi positions	Yes	Yes	Yes
Pi positions from stock	No	No	No

8 Fount storage and retrieval

	600	400	Lasercomp 3000
Image masters in machine	4*	1	2 048
Character capacity	397	400	262 144
Characters per second	35	12	Variable

– = Not applicable to system/information not available

* Plus 100 35mm slides with additional characters

Varityper

	744	748
1 Typesizes		
Minimum typesize	5pt	5pt
Maximum typesize	18pt	72pt
Increment for typesize increase	Fixed sizes	Fixed sizes
2 Letter and interline spacing		
Units to the em	18	18
Plus letterspacing: min/max	1–6 units	1–6 units
Minus letterspacing: min/max	1–6 units	1–6 units
Kerning facility	No	No
Maximum interline spacing	49pt	99pt
Increment for interline spacing	0.5pt	0.5pt
Reverse line-feed	No	No
3 Mixing typefaces and sizes		
Typeface mix within a line	Yes	Yes
Automatic typeface mix	Yes	Yes
Typesize mix within a line	No	Yes
Automatic typesize mix	No	Yes
Typeface/size mix within a line	No	Yes
Baseline alignment	Yes	Yes
Centre alignment	–	–
Top alignment	–	–
4 Output material		
Maximum measure	33 pica ems	45 pica ems
Output on paper	Yes	Yes
Output on film	Yes	Yes
Paper/film widths	102–203mm	102–203mm

– = Not applicable to system/information not available

Compset 560 II	Compset 3560	Compset 4560	CompEdit
5.5pt	5.5pt	5.5pt	5.5pt
74pt	74pt	74pt	74pt
1pt	1pt	1pt	0.5pt
36	36	36	36
0.125 unit–∞	0.125 unit–∞	0.125 unit–∞	0.125 unit–∞
0.125 unit–∞	0.125 unit–∞	0.125 unit–∞	0.125 unit–∞
No	No	No	No
99pt	99pt	99pt	99pt
0.5pt	0.5pt	0.5pt	0.25pt
Yes	Yes	Yes	Yes
Yes	Yes	Yes	Yes
Yes	Yes	Yes	Yes
Yes	Yes	Yes	Yes
Yes	Yes	Yes	Yes
Yes	Yes	Yes	Yes
Yes	Yes	Yes	Yes
Yes	Yes	Yes	Yes
Yes	Yes	Yes	Yes
45 pica ems	70 pica ems	70 pica ems	70 pica ems
Yes	Yes	Yes	Yes
Yes	Yes	Yes	Yes
102–203mm	102–305mm	102–305mm	102–305mm

Varityper

	744	748

5 Hyphenation and tabbing

Input	Paper tape	Paper, Magnetic tape
Unjustified tapes	Yes	Yes
Hyphenless justification	Yes	Yes
Discretionary justification	Yes	Yes
Logic justification	Yes	Yes
Exception dictionary justification	Yes	Yes
Tabular facility	Yes	Yes
Number of tab positions	–	–
Tab: range left	Yes	Yes
Tab: range right	Yes	Yes
Tab: centred	Yes	Yes

6 Rules

Horizontal rules	–	–
Vertical rules	–	–
Box rules	–	–

7 Fount make-up

Image master	Disc	Disc
Founts per master	4	4
Characters per typeface	112	112
Pi positions	No	No
Pi positions from stock	Yes	Yes

8 Fount storage and retrieval

Image masters in machine	1	1
Character capacity	448	448
Characters per second	15	25

– = *Not applicable to system/information not available*

Compset 560 II	Compset 3560	Compset 4560	CompEdit
Floppy diskette	Floppy diskette	Floppy diskette	Floppy diskette
Yes	Yes	Yes	Yes
Yes	Yes	Yes	Yes
Yes	Yes	Yes	Yes
Yes	Yes	Yes	Yes
Yes	Yes	Yes	Yes
Yes	Yes	Yes	Yes
99	99	99	99
Yes	Yes	Yes	Yes
Yes	Yes	Yes	Yes
Yes	Yes	Yes	Yes
Yes	Yes	Yes	Yes
Yes	Yes	Yes	Yes
Yes	Yes	Yes	Yes
Film disc	Film disc	Film disc	Film disc
4	4	4	4
112	112	112	112
No	No	No	No
Yes	Yes	Yes	Yes
4	4	16	16
448	448	1 792	1 792
11	25	25	25

Part IV Typestyles

The tables included on the following pages are intended to assist the user in identifying a single typeface when it is given a variety of names by different manufacturers. For example, by referring to page 208 it can be seen that Optima is alternatively referred to as Chelmsford, Musica, Optimist, OP, Oracle and Zenith. Quite a problem of identification for the designer! The tables should make these alternatives clear; bold face headings and solid bullets indicate the chosen typeface, whereas light face headings and outline bullets indicate alternative references to the same face. Manufacturers holding the typefaces are indicated by bullets under the following abbreviated cross-headings:

AL = Alphatype	HA = Harris Corporation
AU = Autologic	IT = Itek
BE = Berthold	ML = Mergenthaler Linotype
BO = Bobst-Graphic	MO = Monotype
CO = Compugraphic	VA = Varityper
HE = Dr Hell	

It should also be noted that manufacturers' variants of a single typeface will also have different typefactors – see pages 228–287.

Typeface	AL	AU	BE	BO	CO	HE	HA	IT	ML	MO	VA
Abel		●			●						
Ad Bold		●									
Dom					○						
Polka			○								
AG								●			
Avant Garde	○	○	○		○		○		○		○
Akiba		●									
Akzidenz Grotesk			●	●	●						
Albertina										●	
Albion										●	
Aldus						●			●		
Alma		●									
Alpha Gothic	●										
News Gothic		○	○		○					○	○
Trade Gothic									○		
Alphavers		●									
Galaxy						○					
UN							○				
Univers	○	○	○	○	○				○	○	○
Alpin Gothic					●						
Alternate Gothic		○							○		○
Alternate Gothic	●								●		●
Alpin Gothic					○						

	AL	AU	BE	BO	CO	HE	HA	IT	ML	MO	VA
AM								●			
Americana		○							○		
American Classic					○						
Colonial											○

	AL	AU	BE	BO	CO	HE	HA	IT	ML	MO	VA
Americana			●						●		
AM								○			
American Classic					○						
Colonial											○

	AL	AU	BE	BO	CO	HE	HA	IT	ML	MO	VA
American Antique					●						

	AL	AU	BE	BO	CO	HE	HA	IT	ML	MO	VA
American Classic					●						
AM								○			
Americana		○							○		
Colonial											○

	AL	AU	BE	BO	CO	HE	HA	IT	ML	MO	VA
American Typewriter ●					●				●	●	
AT								○			

	AL	AU	BE	BO	CO	HE	HA	IT	ML	MO	VA
American Uncial					●						
Uncial					○						

	AL	AU	BE	BO	CO	HE	HA	IT	ML	MO	VA
Andover			●								●
Elegante							○				
Malibu		○									
Paladium					○						
Palatino		○				○			○		
Patina	○										
PT								○			

	AL	AU	BE	BO	CO	HE	HA	IT	ML	MO	VA
Angeles			●								

AL *Alphatype*   AU *Autologic*   BE *Berthold*   BO *Bobst-Graphic*
CO *Compugraphic*   HE *Dr Hell*   HA *Harris Corporation*   IT *Itek*
ML *Mergenthaler Linotype* MO *Monotype* VA *Varityper*

	AL	AU	BE	BO	CO	HE	HA	IT	ML	MO	VA
Angro						●					
Antique				●					●		
Antique Olive			●	●	●				●		
Olive											○
Antique Open Face									●		
	AL	AU	BE	BO	CO	HE	HA	IT	ML	MO	VA
Anzeigen Grotesk			●								
Aura					○						
Aurora		○									
Apollo											●
Aquarius					●						
Arabic Script					●						
	AL	AU	BE	BO	CO	HE	HA	IT	ML	MO	VA
Ariston			●								
Arkona			●								
Armenian					●						
Artcraft					●						
AS										●	
Ascot Mediaeval			●								
	AL	AU	BE	BO	CO	HE	HA	IT	ML	MO	VA
Aster			●	●	●	●			●		
Astro		○									
Aztec			○								

	AL	AU	BE	BO	CO	HE	HA	IT	ML	MO	VA
Astro	●										
Aster			O	O	O	O			O		
Aztec		O									

	AL	AU	BE	BO	CO	HE	HA	IT	ML	MO	VA
AT								●			
American Typewriter		O			O				O	O	

	AL	AU	BE	BO	CO	HE	HA	IT	ML	MO	VA
Atlantic	●										
PL								O			
Plantin			O	O	O	O			O	O	O

	AL	AU	BE	BO	CO	HE	HA	IT	ML	MO	VA
Augustea			●								

	AL	AU	BE	BO	CO	HE	HA	IT	ML	MO	VA
Aura					●						
Anzeigen Grotesk		O									
Aurora	O										

	AL	AU	BE	BO	CO	HE	HA	IT	ML	MO	VA
Auriga									●		

	AL	AU	BE	BO	CO	HE	HA	IT	ML	MO	VA
Aurora (AL)	●										
Anzeigen Grotesk		O									
Aura					O						

	AL	AU	BE	BO	CO	HE	HA	IT	ML	MO	VA
Aurora (ML)									●		●
Empira	O	O									O
News No 2, 12					O						
Regal							O				
RG								O			

	AL	AU	BE	BO	CO	HE	HA	IT	ML	MO	VA
Avant Garde	●	●		●					●		●
AG								O			

	AL	AU	BE	BO	CO	HE	HA	IT	ML	MO	VA
Aztec		●									
Aster			O	O	O	O			O		
Astro	O										

	AL	AU	BE	BO	CO	HE	HA	IT	ML	MO	VA
Ballardvale		●									
Hanover											○
Mallard				○							
ME							○				
Medallion						○					
Melior			○							○	○
Uranus	○										

	AL	AU	BE	BO	CO	HE	HA	IT	ML	MO	VA
Balmoral		●									

	AL	AU	BE	BO	CO	HE	HA	IT	ML	MO	VA
Bank Gothic									●		
De Luxe Gothic					○						

	AL	AU	BE	BO	CO	HE	HA	IT	ML	MO	VA
Basilia				●							

	AL	AU	BE	BO	CO	HE	HA	IT	ML	MO	VA
Baskerline	●										
Baskerville		○	○	○	○	○	○		○	○	○
BK								○			

	AL	AU	BE	BO	CO	HE	HA	IT	ML	MO	VA
Baskerville		●	●	●	●	●	●		●	●	●
Baskerline	○										
BK								○			

	AL	AU	BE	BO	CO	HE	HA	IT	ML	MO	VA
Basque					●						

	AL	AU	BE	BO	CO	HE	HA	IT	ML	MO	VA
Bauhaus			●	●	●				●		
BH								○			

	AL	AU	BE	BO	CO	HE	HA	IT	ML	MO	VA
BE								●			

	AL	AU	BE	BO	CO	HE	HA	IT	ML	MO	VA
Bedford		●									
Imperial							○				
News No 4					○						

	AL	AU	BE	BO	CO	HE	HA	IT	ML	MO	VA
Bell Gothic		●							●	●	

	AL	AU	BE	BO	CO	HE	HA	IT	ML	MO	VA
Belmont		●									
Bem					●						
Bembo		○	○	○		○			○	○	○
Griffo	○										
Bembo		●	●	●		●			●	●	●
Bem					○						
Griffo	○										

	AL	AU	BE	BO	CO	HE	HA	IT	ML	MO	VA
Benguiat			●		●						
BG								○			
Berliner Grotesk			●								
Bernase Roman					●						
Berner											●
Sabon			○						○	○	
Sybil		○									

	AL	AU	BE	BO	CO	HE	HA	IT	ML	MO	VA
Bernhard			●								
Liberty					○						
Lotus						○					
Berthold Script			●								
BG								●			
Benguiat			○		○						

	AL	AU	BE	BO	CO	HE	HA	IT	ML	MO	VA
BH								●			
Bauhaus			○	○	○				○		
Binney Old Style									●	●	

	AL	AU	BE	BO	CO	HE	HA	IT	ML	MO	VA
BK								●			
Baskerline	O										
Baskerville		O	O	O	O	O	O		O	O	O
BL								●			
Blado										●	
Blizzard						●					
BM								●			
Bookman		O	O		O				O	O	
BO								●			
Bodoni		O	O	O	O	O			O	O	O
Bodoni		●	●	●	●	●			●	●	●
BO								O			
Bolt Bold					●						
Book					●						
Bookman		●	●		●				●	●	
BM								O			
BR								●			
Brush		O			O						O
Branding Iron					●						
Broadway		●									
Brody											●
Brophy Script					O						

	AL	AU	BE	BO	CO	HE	HA	IT	ML	MO	VA
Brophy Script					●						
Brody											○
Bruce Old Style									●	●	
Brush		●			●						●
BR							○				
Busorama					●						

	AL	AU	BE	BO	CO	HE	HA	IT	ML	MO	VA
Cairo							●				
Memphis			○						○		
Rockwell			○	○	○					○	
ST								○			
Stymie	○	○			○						○

	AL	AU	BE	BO	CO	HE	HA	IT	ML	MO	VA
Caledo	●										
Caledonia			○						○	○	
California					○						
CD								○			
Highland		○									○
Laurel							○				

	AL	AU	BE	BO	CO	HE	HA	IT	ML	MO	VA
Caledonia			●						●	●	
Caledo	○										
California					○						
CD								○			
Highland		○									○
Laurel							○				

	AL	AU	BE	BO	CO	HE	HA	IT	ML	MO	VA
California					●						
Caledo	○										
Caledonia			○						○	○	
CD								○			
Highland		○									○
Laurel							○				

	AL	AU	BE	BO	CO	HE	HA	IT	ML	MO	VA
Caliope Antique					●						
Calvert										●	
Camelot					●						●
EX								○			
Excelsior		○							○	○	
News No 14					○						
	AL	AU	BE	BO	CO	HE	HA	IT	ML	MO	VA
Candida			●	●	●	●			●	●	
Caprice			●								
Cartier					●						
Cascade									●		
	AL	AU	BE	BO	CO	HE	HA	IT	ML	MO	VA
Caslon	●	●			●				●		
CL								○			
CC								●			
Coronet		○			○						
	AL	AU	BE	BO	CO	HE	HA	IT	ML	MO	VA
CD								●			
Caledo	○										
Caledonia			○						○	○	
California					○						
Highland		○									○
Laurel							○				
	AL	AU	BE	BO	CO	HE	HA	IT	ML	MO	VA
CE								●			
Century		○	○	○	○	○	○		○	○	○
Century X	○										
Celestina			●								

	AL	AU	BE	BO	CO	HE	HA	IT	ML	MO	VA
Century		●	●	●	●	●	●		●	●	●
CE								O			
Century X	O										
Century Old Style		●			●				●	●	
	AL	AU	BE	BO	CO	HE	HA	IT	ML	MO	VA
Century Schoolbook		●	●	●		●	●		●	●	
Century Text	O										
Century Textbook					O						
CS								O			
Schoolbook											O
	AL	AU	BE	BO	CO	HE	HA	IT	ML	MO	VA
Century Text	●										
Century Schoolbook		O	O	O		O	O		O	O	
Century Textbook					O						
CS								O			
Schoolbook											O
	AL	AU	BE	BO	CO	HE	HA	IT	ML	MO	VA
Century Textbook					●						
Century Schoolbook		O	O	O		O	O		O	O	
Century Text	O										
CS								O			
Schoolbook											O
	AL	AU	BE	BO	CO	HE	HA	IT	ML	MO	VA
Century X	●										
CE								O			
Century		O	O	O	O	O	O		O	O	O
	AL	AU	BE	BO	CO	HE	HA	IT	ML	MO	VA
CH				●				●			
Cheltenham	O	O	O		O				O		O
Cheltonian							O				
Gloucester										O	
Nordhoff		O									

PHOTOCOMPOSITION TYPEFACES

	AL	AU	BE	BO	CO	HE	HA	IT	ML	MO	VA
Chatsworth		●									
Chelmsford		●									●
Musica	○										
OP								○			
Optima			○							○	○
Optimist		○									
Oracle					○						
Zenith							○				
Chelsea		●									
Gothic No 2, 3					○						
Metro									○		
Cheltenham	●	●	●		●				●		●
CH				○			○				
Cheltonian						○					
Gloucester										○	
Nordhoff		○									
Cheltonian							●				
CH				○			○				
Cheltenham	○	○	○		○				○		○
Gloucester										○	
Nordhoff		○									
Chisel							●				
City		●									
CL							●				
Caslon		○	○		○				○		

AL *Alphatype*   AU *Autologic*   BE *Berthold*   BO *Bobst-Graphic*
CO *Compugraphic*   HE *Dr Hell*   HA *Harris Corporation*   IT *Itek*
ML *Mergenthaler Linotype*   MO *Monotype*   VA *Varityper*

	AL	AU	BE	BO	CO	HE	HA	IT	ML	MO	VA
Clarendon	●		●	●	●	●			●	●	●
Clarion		○									
Clarique						○					
CN								○			

Clarinda Typewriter									●		
	AL	AU	BE	BO	CO	HE	HA	IT	ML	MO	VA
Clarion		●									
Clarendon	○		○	○	○	○			○	○	○
Clarique						○					
CN								○			

	AL	AU	BE	BO	CO	HE	HA	IT	ML	MO	VA
Claro	●										
Geneva		○									
HE								○			
Helios				○							
Helvetica			○						○	○	
Megaron											○
Newton		○									
Vega							○				

	AL	AU	BE	BO	CO	HE	HA	IT	ML	MO	VA
Clarique							●				
Clarendon	○		○	○	○	○			○	○	○
Clarion		○									
CN								○			

Clearface			●		●						

Cloister		●			●				●		
	AL	AU	BE	BO	CO	HE	HA	IT	ML	MO	VA
CN								●			
Clarendon	○		○	○	○				○	○	○
Clarion		○									
Clarique							○				

CO								●			
Copperplate					O						
Copperplate Gothic									O		O

Colonia						●					
	AL	AU	BE	BO	CO	HE	HA	IT	ML	MO	VA

Colonial											●
AM								O			
Americana			O						O		
American Classic					O						

Comenius			●								
	AL	AU	BE	BO	CO	HE	HA	IT	ML	MO	VA

Command		●									
	AL	AU	BE	BO	CO	HE	HA	IT	ML	MO	VA

Commercial Script				●							

Computer				●							

Concorde			●								

Condensed				●							
	AL	AU	BE	BO	CO	HE	HA	IT	ML	MO	VA

Continental							●				
Mediaeval											O
Olympus	O										
Saul		O									
Trump Mediaeval			O		O	O			O		
	AL	AU	BE	BO	CO	HE	HA	IT	ML	MO	VA

Cooper Black	●	◉	●		●					●	●
CP								O			
Pabst									O		

AL *Alphatype*   AU *Autologic*   BE *Berthold*   BO *Bobst-Graphic*
CO *Compugraphic*   HE *Dr Hell*   HA *Harris Corporation*   IT *Itek*
ML *Mergenthaler Linotype* MO *Monotype* VA *Varityper*

	AL	AU	BE	BO	CO	HE	HA	IT	ML	MO	VA
Copperplate					●						
CO									○		
Copperplate Gothic										○	○

	AL	AU	BE	BO	CO	HE	HA	IT	ML	MO	VA
Copperplate Gothic									●		●
CO								○			
Copperplate					○						

	AL	AU	BE	BO	CO	HE	HA	IT	ML	MO	VA
Corinth		●									
Doric		○							○		
IC								○			
Ionic				○					○	○	
News Text (MED)	○										

	AL	AU	BE	BO	CO	HE	HA	IT	ML	MO	VA
Corona									●		
CR								○			
Crown		○									○
Koronna	○										
News No 3, 5, 6				○							
Nimbus		○									
Royal							○				

	AL	AU	BE	BO	CO	HE	HA	IT	ML	MO	VA
Coronet		●			●						
CC								○			

	AL	AU	BE	BO	CO	HE	HA	IT	ML	MO	VA
Corvinus			●								

	AL	AU	BE	BO	CO	HE	HA	IT	ML	MO	VA
CP								●			
Cooper Black	○	○	○		○					○	○
Pabst									○		

AL *Alphatype*   AU *Autologic*   BE *Berthold*   BO *Bobst-Graphic*
CO *Compugraphic*   HE *Dr Hell*   HA *Harris Corporation*   IT *Itek*
ML *Mergenthaler Linotype*   MO *Monotype*   VA *Varityper*

	AL	AU	BE	BO	CO	HE	HA	IT	ML	MO	VA
CR								●			
Corona									○		
Crown		○									○
Koronna	○										
News No 3, 5, 6					○						
Nimbus		○									
Royal							○				
Craw Modern									●		

	AL	AU	BE	BO	CO	HE	HA	IT	ML	MO	VA
Crown		●									●
CR								○			
Corona									○		
Koronna	○										
News No 3, 5, 6					○						
Nimbus		○									
Royal							○				
CRT Gothic									●		

	AL	AU	BE	BO	CO	HE	HA	IT	ML	MO	VA
CS								●			
Century Schoolbook	○	○	○		○	○			○	○	
Century Text		○									
Century Textbook					○						
Schoolbook											○
Cyrillic				●							

	AL	AU	BE	BO	CO	HE	HA	IT	ML	MO	VA
Deepdene											●
Delia							●				
Delmar		●									

	AL	AU	BE	BO	CO	HE	HA	IT	ML	MO	VA
De Luxe Gothic							●				
Bank Gothic									○		
Demos					●						
Devinne									●		
Didi				●							
Digi						●					

	AL	AU	BE	BO	CO	HE	HA	IT	ML	MO	VA
Digiset			●								
Directory Gothic				●							
Diskus			●								
Dom					●						
Ad Bold		○									
Polka			○								

	AL	AU	BE	BO	CO	HE	HA	IT	ML	MO	VA
Dominante			●	●							
Doric		●							●		
Corinth		○									
IC								○			
Ionic				○						○	○
News Text (MED)	○										

	AL	AU	BE	BO	CO	HE	HA	IT	ML	MO	VA
Dow News		●									
Ideal								○			
News No 9				○							
Durante		●									

	AL	AU	BE	BO	CO	HE	HA	IT	ML	MO	VA
Dutch Old Style					●						

	AL	AU	BE	BO	CO	HE	HA	IT	ML	MO	VA
Eccentric					●						
Edelweiss	●										
Weiss			○		○				○		
Edison						●					
Egizio			●	●							

	AL	AU	BE	BO	CO	HE	HA	IT	ML	MO	VA
Egyptian					●				●	●	
Egyptienne			●	●							
Ehrhardt			●	●							●
Elante					●						
Electra									○		
Selectra		○									

	AL	AU	BE	BO	CO	HE	HA	IT	ML	MO	VA
Electra									●		
Elante					○						
Selectra		○									

	AL	AU	BE	BO	CO	HE	HA	IT	ML	MO	VA
Elegante							●				
Andover		○									○
Malibu		○									
Paladium					○						
Palatino			○				○		○		
Patina	○										
PT									○		

AL *Alphatype*   AU *Autologic*   BE *Berthold*   BO *Bobst-Graphic*
CO *Compugraphic*   HE *Dr Hell*   HA *Harris Corporation*   IT *Itek*
ML *Mergenthaler Linotype*   MO *Monotype*   VA *Varityper*

	AL	AU	BE	BO	CO	HE	HA	IT	ML	MO	VA
Embassy							●				
Florentine Script					○						
Helanna Script											○

	AL	AU	BE	BO	CO	HE	HA	IT	ML	MO	VA
Empira	●	●									●
Aurora										○	○
News No 2, 12					○						
Regal							○				
RG								○			

	AL	AU	BE	BO	CO	HE	HA	IT	ML	MO	VA
Englische Schreibschrift			●	●							

	AL	AU	BE	BO	CO	HE	HA	IT	ML	MO	VA
English	●										
English Times					○						
Times						○					
Times New 2				○							
Times New Roman			○								
Times Roman		○					○		○	○	○
TR								○			

	AL	AU	BE	BO	CO	HE	HA	IT	ML	MO	VA
English Times					●						
English	○										
Times						○					
Times No 2				○							
Times New Roman			○								
Times Roman		○					○		○	○	○
TR								○			

	AL	AU	BE	BO	CO	HE	HA	IT	ML	MO	VA
Engravers					●				●		
Engravers Old English	○									○	

	AL	AU	BE	BO	CO	HE	HA	IT	ML	MO	VA
Engravers Old English	●									●	
Engravers					○				○		

	AL	AU	BE	BO	CO	HE	HA	IT	ML	MO	VA
Eras			●						●		

	AL	AU	BE	BO	CO	HE	HA	IT	ML	MO	VA
Erbar					●				●		

	AL	AU	BE	BO	CO	HE	HA	IT	ML	MO	VA
ES								●			
Eurogothic	○										
Eurostile			○							○	○
Microstyle					○						

	AL	AU	BE	BO	CO	HE	HA	IT	ML	MO	VA
Euclid					●						

	AL	AU	BE	BO	CO	HE	HA	IT	ML	MO	VA
Eurogothic	●										
ES								○			
Eurostile			○							○	○
Microstyle					○						

	AL	AU	BE	BO	CO	HE	HA	IT	ML	MO	VA
Eurostile			●						●		●
ES								○			
Eurogothic	○										
Microstyle					○						

	AL	AU	BE	BO	CO	HE	HA	IT	ML	MO	VA
EX								●			
Camelot					○						○
Excelsior		○							○	○	
News No 14					○						

	AL	AU	BE	BO	CO	HE	HA	IT	ML	MO	VA
Excelsior		●							●	●	
Camelot					○						○
EX								○			
News No 14					○						

	AL	AU	BE	BO	CO	HE	HA	IT	ML	MO	VA
Fairfield									●		

AL *Alphatype*   AU *Autologic*   BE *Berthold*   BO *Bobst-Graphic*
CO *Compugraphic*   HE *Dr Hell*   HA *Harris Corporation*   IT *Itek*
ML *Mergenthaler Linotype* MO *Monotype* VA *Varityper*

	AL	AU	BE	BO	CO	HE	HA	IT	ML	MO	VA
Falstaff										●	
Fat Face				●							
Federal Antique				●							
Fenice			●								
Figaro										●	
Firenze				●							
FL								●			
Flange			●								
Flemish Script					●						
Florentine Script					●						
Embassy						○					
Helanna Script											○
Floridian Script					●						
Nuptial									○		
Flyer			●								
Folio			●		●					●	
Forte										●	
Fournier										●	
Franklin			●		●						
Franklin Gothic	○	○							○		○

	AL	AU	BE	BO	CO	HE	HA	IT	ML	MO	VA
Franklin Gothic		●	●						●		●
Franklin			○		○						
French Script					●						
Kaylin Script											○
French Round Face										●	
Fritz Quadrata		●	●		●				●		
FZ								○			
Frutiger										●	
FU								●			
Futura	○		○	○	○	○	○		○		
Photura		○									
Spartan									○		
Techno		○									○
Twentieth Century										○	
Futura	●		●	●	●	●	●		●		
FU								○			
Photura		○									
Spartan									○		
Techno		○									○
Twentieth Century										○	
Futura 5½pt							●				
Sans 5½/6pt					○						
Spartan									○		
Techno Book		○									○
FZ								●			
Fritz Quadrata	○	○			○				○		

	AL	AU	BE	BO	CO	HE	HA	IT	ML	MO	VA
Galaxy							●				
Alphavers	○										
UN								○			
Univers		○	○	○	○	○			○	○	○
Gando Ronde									●		

	AL	AU	BE	BO	CO	HE	HA	IT	ML	MO	VA
Garamond		●	●	●	●	●			●	●	●
GD							○				
Garamont			●			●					
Garth Graphic				●							
GD								●			
Garamond		○	○	○	○	○			○	○	○

	AL	AU	BE	BO	CO	HE	HA	IT	ML	MO	VA
Geneva		●									
Claro	○										
HE								○			
Helios					○						
Helvetica			○						○	○	
Megaron											○
Newton		○									
Vega							○				

	AL	AU	BE	BO	CO	HE	HA	IT	ML	MO	VA
Geometric				●							
Gill Sans			●	●	●	●			●	●	
Glib	○										

	AL	AU	BE	BO	CO	HE	HA	IT	ML	MO	VA
Gill Kayo		●									
Glenn Shaded				●							

	AL	AU	BE	BO	CO	HE	HA	IT	ML	MO	VA
Glib	●										
Gill Sans			○	○	○	○			○	○	
Gloucester										●	
CH				○			○				
Cheltenham	○	○	○		○				○		○
Cheltonian							○				
Nordhoff		○									
	AL	AU	BE	BO	CO	HE	HA	IT	ML	MO	VA
GO							●				
Goudy		○	○		○				○	○	
Gold Nugget				●							
Gold Rush			○								
	AL	AU	BE	BO	CO	HE	HA	IT	ML	MO	VA
Gold Rush			●								
Gold Nugget					○						
Gorilla				●							
Gothic		●			●				●		
	AL	AU	BE	BO	CO	HE	HA	IT	ML	MO	VA
Gothic No 2, 3				●							
Chelsea		○									
Metro									○		
Gothic Outline											●
Goudy		●	●		●				●	●	
GO								○			
	AL	AU	BE	BO	CO	HE	HA	IT	ML	MO	VA
Granite		●									
Lisbon					○						
Lydian			○				○				

	AL	AU	BE	BO	CO	HE	HA	IT	ML	MO	VA
Greek		●			●						
Griechisch						●					
Griffo	●										
BEM					○						
Bembo		○	○	○	○				○	○	○
Grizzly					●						
Grotesk Negative					●						
Grotesque										●	
Monotype Grotesque						○					
Grouch					●						
Hanover											●
Ballardvale		○									
Mallard				○							
ME								○			
Medallion							○				
Melior			○						○	○	
Uranus	○										
Haverhill											●
HE								●			
Claro	○										
Geneva		○									
Helios					○						
Helvetica			○						○	○	
Megaron											○
Newton		○									
Vega							○				

	AL	AU	BE	BO	CO	HE	HA	IT	ML	MO	VA
Headline										●	
Headline Bodoni		●									
Helanna Script											●
Embassy							○				
Florentine Script				○							
Heldustry					●						

	AL	AU	BE	BO	CO	HE	HA	IT	ML	MO	VA
Helios					●						
Claro	○										
Geneva		○									
HE							○				
Helvetica			○						○	○	
Megaron											○
Newton		○									
Vega								○			

	AL	AU	BE	BO	CO	HE	HA	IT	ML	MO	VA
Helvetica			●						●	●	
Claro	○										
Geneva		○									
HE							○				
Helios					○						
Megaron											○
Newton		○									
Vega						○					

	AL	AU	BE	BO	CO	HE	HA	IT	ML	MO	VA
Heraldus					●						

AL *Alphatype*   AU *Autologic*   BE *Berthold*   BO *Bobst-Graphic*
CO *Compugraphic*   HE *Dr Hell*   HA *Harris Corporation*   IT *Itek*
ML *Mergenthaler Linotype* MO *Monotype* VA *Varityper*

	AL	AU	BE	BO	CO	HE	HA	IT	ML	MO	VA
Highland		●									●
Caledo	○										
Caledonia			○						○	○	
California					○						
CD								○			
Laurel							○				

	AL	AU	BE	BO	CO	HE	HA	IT	ML	MO	VA
Hobo			●	●					●		
Tramp		○									

	AL	AU	BE	BO	CO	HE	HA	IT	ML	MO	VA
Holland				●							

| **Hollandese Mediaeval** | | | | ● | | | | | | | |

	AL	AU	BE	BO	CO	HE	HA	IT	ML	MO	VA
Holsatia						●					

| **Honda** | | | | | ● | | | | | | |

| **Hopson** | | ● | | | | | | | | | |

| **Horley** | | | ● | ● | | | | | | | |

	AL	AU	BE	BO	CO	HE	HA	IT	ML	MO	VA
IB (Itek Bookface)								●			

	AL	AU	BE	BO	CO	HE	HA	IT	ML	MO	VA
IC								●			
Corinth		○									
Doric		○							○		
Ionic				○					○	○	
News Text (MED)	○										

	AL	AU	BE	BO	CO	HE	HA	IT	ML	MO	VA
ID (Itek Directory)								●			

	AL	AU	BE	BO	CO	HE	HA	IT	ML	MO	VA
Ideal							●				
Dow News		○									
News No 9					○						

	AL	AU	BE	BO	CO	HE	HA	IT	ML	MO	VA
IK (Itek Blackletter)								●			
Imperial								●			
Bedford		O									
News No 4					O						
Impress		●									
Impressum			●		●	●					
Imprint			●						●	●	
Impuls			●								
Inflex										●	
Ionic				●					●	●	
Corinth		O									
Doric		O							O		
IC								O			
News Text (MED)	O										
Iridium									●		
Isabella				●							
Italia			●	●							
Italian Old Style			●								
JA								●			
Janson										O	O

AL *Alphatype*   AU *Autologic*   BE *Berthold*   BO *Bobst-Graphic*
CO *Compugraphic*   HE *Dr Hell*   HA *Harris Corporation*   IT *Itek*
ML *Mergenthaler Linotype* MO *Monotype* VA *Varityper*

PHOTOCOMPOSITION TYPEFACES

	AL	AU	BE	BO	CO	HE	HA	IT	ML	MO	VA
Janson									●		●
JA								○			
Jay Gothic		●									
Jones Antique		●									

	AL	AU	BE	BO	CO	HE	HA	IT	ML	MO	VA
Kabel			●		●				●		●
KL								○			
Kapitellia						●					

	AL	AU	BE	BO	CO	HE	HA	IT	ML	MO	VA
Kaylin Script											●
French Script				○							

	AL	AU	BE	BO	CO	HE	HA	IT	ML	MO	VA
Kennerley					●						
Kenntonian							○				
Kensington		○									

	AL	AU	BE	BO	CO	HE	HA	IT	ML	MO	VA
Kenntonian							●				
Kennerley					○						
Kensington		○									

	AL	AU	BE	BO	CO	HE	HA	IT	ML	MO	VA
Kensington		●									
Kennerley					○						
Kenntonian							○				

	AL	AU	BE	BO	CO	HE	HA	IT	ML	MO	VA
KL								●			
Kabel		○		○					○		○
Klang										●	

	AL	AU	BE	BO	CO	HE	HA	IT	ML	MO	VA
KN								●			
Korrina			○	○	○					○	○

	AL	AU	BE	BO	CO	HE	HA	IT	ML	MO	VA
Koronna	●										
Corona									○		
CR								○			
Crown		○									○
News No 3, 5, 6					○						
Nimbus		○									
Royal							○				
	AL	AU	BE	BO	CO	HE	HA	IT	ML	MO	VA
Korrina			●	●	●				●		●
KN								○			
	AL	AU	BE	BO	CO	HE	HA	IT	ML	MO	VA
La Script		●									
Latine		●									
Meridien			○						○		
MD								○			
Latin					●						
	AL	AU	BE	BO	CO	HE	HA	IT	ML	MO	VA
Laurel							●				
Caledo	○										
Caledonia			○						○	○	
California					○						
CD								○			
Highland		○									○
LE (Lectura)								●			
LG								●			
Lubalin Graph			○		○				○		
	AL	AU	BE	BO	CO	HE	HA	IT	ML	MO	VA
Liberty					●						
Bernhard		○									
Lotus							○				

	AL	AU	BE	BO	CO	HE	HA	IT	ML	MO	VA
Libra					●						
Libretto	○										
Libretto	●										
Libra					○						
Life			●								
	AL	AU	BE	BO	CO	HE	HA	IT	ML	MO	VA
Lightline Gothic			●								
Linoscript									●		
Linotext									●		
	AL	AU	BE	BO	CO	HE	HA	IT	ML	MO	VA
Lisbon					●						
Granite		○									
Lydian			○				○				
London Text			●		●						
Lorraine		●									
Venetian Script					○						
	AL	AU	BE	BO	CO	HE	HA	IT	ML	MO	VA
Lotus							●				
Bernhard		○									
Liberty					○						
Lubalin Graph			●		●				●		
LG								○			
Luce				●							
	AL	AU	BE	BO	CO	HE	HA	IT	ML	MO	VA
Lydian			●				●				
Granite		○									
Lisbon					○						

	AL	AU	BE	BO	CO	HE	HA	IT	ML	MO	VA
Machine					●						
Madison			●								
Malibu		●									
Andover		O									O
Elegante						O					
Paladium					O						
Palatino			O			O				O	
Patina	O										
PT								O			

	AL	AU	BE	BO	CO	HE	HA	IT	ML	MO	VA
Mallard					●						
Ballardvale		O									
Hanover											O
ME							O				
Medallion						O					
Melior			O							O	O
Uranus	O										

	AL	AU	BE	BO	CO	HE	HA	IT	ML	MO	VA
Manhattan					●						
Marconi					●						
McCollough					●						

	AL	AU	BE	BO	CO	HE	HA	IT	ML	MO	VA
MD								●			
Latine		O									
Meridien			O						O		

AL *Alphatype*   AU *Autologic*   BE *Berthold*   BO *Bobst-Graphic*
CO *Compugraphic*   HE *Dr Hell*   HA *Harris Corporation*   IT *Itek*
ML *Mergenthaler Linotype* MO *Monotype* VA *Varityper*

	AL	AU	BE	BO	CO	HE	HA	IT	ML	MO	VA
ME								●			
Ballardvale		○									
Hanover											○
Mallard					○						
Medallion							○				
Melior			○						○	○	
Uranus	○										

Mead		●									

	AL	AU	BE	BO	CO	HE	HA	IT	ML	MO	VA
Medallion							●				
Ballardvale		○									
Hanover											○
Mallard					○						
ME								○			
Melior			○						○	○	
Uranus	○										

Media				●							

	AL	AU	BE	BO	CO	HE	HA	IT	ML	MO	VA
Mediaeval											●
Continental						○					
Olympus	○										
Saul		○									
Trump Mediaeval			○		○	○		○			

Medici									●		

	AL	AU	BE	BO	CO	HE	HA	IT	ML	MO	VA
Megaron											●
Claro	○										
Geneva		○									
HE							○				
Helios					○						
Helvetica			○						○	○	
Newton		○									
Vega							○				

PHOTOCOMPOSITION TYPEFACES

	AL	AU	BE	BO	CO	HE	HA	IT	ML	MO	VA
Melior			●						●	●	
Ballardvale		○									
Hanover											○
Mallard					○						
ME								○			
Medallion							○				
Uranus	○										
Mellis		●									
	AL	AU	BE	BO	CO	HE	HA	IT	ML	MO	VA
Memphis			●						●		
Cairo						○					
Rockwell			○	○	○					○	
ST								○			
Stymie	○	○			○						○
	AL	AU	BE	BO	CO	HE	HA	IT	ML	MO	VA
Meridien			●						●		
Latine		○									
MD								○			
Metabold			●								
Meteor			●								
	AL	AU	BE	BO	CO	HE	HA	IT	ML	MO	VA
Metro									●		
Chelsea		○									
Gothic No 2, 3					○						
Microstyle					●						
ES								○			
Eurogothic	○										
Eurostile			○							○	○
	AL	AU	BE	BO	CO	HE	HA	IT	ML	MO	VA
Milano Roman					●						

	AL	AU	BE	BO	CO	HE	HA	IT	ML	MO	VA
Minuet							●				
Piranesi					○						
Mique					●						
Modern		●							●	●	
Modern Blackletter					○						
Modern Blackletter					●						
Modern		○							○	○	
Monanti						●					
Monoline Script										●	
Monotype Grotesque									●		
Grotesque										○	
Monticello								●			
Morges				●							
Murray					●						
Murray Hill		○									
Murray Hill			●								
Murray					○						
Musica	●										
Chelmsford		○									○
OP								○			
Optima			○						○	○	
Optimist		○									
Oracle					○						
Zenith							○				

	AL	AU	BE	BO	CO	HE	HA	IT	ML	MO	VA
Napoleon						●					
Neo Didot										●	
Neon					●						
Neuzit		●							●	●	

	AL	AU	BE	BO	CO	HE	HA	IT	ML	MO	VA
New Bostonian					●						
New Clarendon										●	
News Gothic		●	●		●		●			●	●
Alpha Gothic	○										
Trade Gothic									○		

	AL	AU	BE	BO	CO	HE	HA	IT	ML	MO	VA
News No 2, 12					●						
Aurora									○		○
Empira	○	○									○
Regal							○				
RG								○			

	AL	AU	BE	BO	CO	HE	HA	IT	ML	MO	VA
News No 3, 5, 6					●						
Coronna									○		
CR								○			
Crown			○								○
Koronna	○										
Nimbus			○								
Royal							○				

	AL	AU	BE	BO	CO	HE	HA	IT	ML	MO	VA
News No 4					●						
Bedford			○								
Imperial							○				

AL *Alphatype* AU *Autologic* BE *Berthold* BO *Bobst-Graphic*
CO *Compugraphic* HE *Dr Hell* HA *Harris Corporation* IT *Itek*
ML *Mergenthaler Linotype* MO *Monotype* VA *Varityper*
PHOTOCOMPOSITION TYPEFACES

	AL	AU	BE	BO	CO	HE	HA	IT	ML	MO	VA
News No 9					●						
Dow News		○									
Ideal							○				

	AL	AU	BE	BO	CO	HE	HA	IT	ML	MO	VA
News No 14					●						
Camelot					○						○
EX								○			
Excelsior		○							○	○	

	AL	AU	BE	BO	CO	HE	HA	IT	ML	MO	VA
News Plantin										●	

	AL	AU	BE	BO	CO	HE	HA	IT	ML	MO	VA
News Text Medium	●										
Corinth		○									
Doric		○									
IC								○			
Ionic				○					○	○	

	AL	AU	BE	BO	CO	HE	HA	IT	ML	MO	VA
Newtext			●		●				●		
NT								○			

	AL	AU	BE	BO	CO	HE	HA	IT	ML	MO	VA
Newton		●									
Claro	○										
Geneva		○									
HE								○			
Helios					○						
Helvetica		○							○	○	
Megaron											○
Vega							○				

	AL	AU	BE	BO	CO	HE	HA	IT	ML	MO	VA
NG								●			

Nikis					●						

AL *Alphatype*　　AU *Autologic*　　BE *Berthold*　　BO *Bobst-Graphic*
CO *Compugraphic*　　HE *Dr Hell*　　HA *Harris Corporation*　　IT *Itek*
ML *Mergenthaler Linotype*　MO *Monotype*　VA *Varityper*

PHOTOCOMPOSITION TYPEFACES

	AL	AU	BE	BO	CO	HE	HA	IT	ML	MO	VA
Nimbus		●									
Coronna									O		
CR								O			
Crown		O									O
Koronna	O										
News No 3, 5, 6					O						
Royal							O				

	AL	AU	BE	BO	CO	HE	HA	IT	ML	MO	VA
Nordhoff		●									
CH				O			O				
Cheltenham	O	O	O		O				O		O
Cheltonian								O			
Gloucester										O	

	AL	AU	BE	BO	CO	HE	HA	IT	ML	MO	VA
Nork					●						
Novarese					●						
Novelta				●							
NT								●			
Newtext			O		O				O		

	AL	AU	BE	BO	CO	HE	HA	IT	ML	MO	VA
Number 21								●			
Nuptial								●			
Floridian Script					O						
Nyon				●							

	AL	AU	BE	BO	CO	HE	HA	IT	ML	MO	VA
OCR-B						●					
Octavian										●	
Old Style		●							●	●	

	AL	AU	BE	BO	CO	HE	HA	IT	ML	MO	VA
Old English		●			●						
Old English Text										○	
Old English Text											●
Old English		○			○						

	AL	AU	BE	BO	CO	HE	HA	IT	ML	MO	VA
Olive											●
Antique Olive			○	○	○				○		
Olympia							●				
Olympian										●	

	AL	AU	BE	BO	CO	HE	HA	IT	ML	MO	VA
Olympus	●										
Continental						○					
Mediaeval											○
Saul		○									
Trump Mediaeval			○		○	○			○		

	AL	AU	BE	BO	CO	HE	HA	IT	ML	MO	VA
OP								●			
Chelmsford		○									○
Musica	○										
Optima			○						○	○	
Optimist		○									
Oracle					○						
Zenith							○				

	AL	AU	BE	BO	CO	HE	HA	IT	ML	MO	VA
Optima			●						●	●	
Chelmsford		○									○
Musica	○										
OP								○			
Optimist		○									
Oracle					○						
Zenith							○				

	AL	AU	BE	BO	CO	HE	HA	IT	ML	MO	VA
Optimist		●									
Chelmsford		O									O
Musica	O										
OP								O			
Optima			O						O	O	
Oracle					O						
Zenith							O				
	AL	AU	BE	BO	CO	HE	HA	IT	ML	MO	VA
Oracle					●						
Chelmsford		O									O
Musica	O										
OP								O			
Optima			O						O	O	
Optimist		O									
Zenith							O				
	AL	AU	BE	BO	CO	HE	HA	IT	ML	MO	VA
Original Script					●						
Orion									●		
	AL	AU	BE	BO	CO	HE	HA	IT	ML	MO	VA
PA								●			
Park Avenue					O				O		O
Pabst									●		
Cooper Black	O	O	O		O					O	O
CP						O					
	AL	AU	BE	BO	CO	HE	HA	IT	ML	MO	VA
Packard					●						
Paddock		●									

AL *Alphatype*   AU *Autologic*   BE *Berthold*   BO *Bobst-Graphic*
CO *Compugraphic*   HE *Dr Hell*   HA *Harris Corporation*   IT *Itek*
ML *Mergenthaler Linotype*   MO *Monotype*   VA *Varityper*

	AL	AU	BE	BO	CO	HE	HA	IT	ML	MO	VA
Paladium					●						
Andover		○									○
Elegante						○					
Malibu		○									
Palatino			○			○			○		
Patina	○										
PT								○			

	AL	AU	BE	BO	CO	HE	HA	IT	ML	MO	VA
Palatino			●			●			●		
Andover		○									○
Elegante						○					
Malibu		○									
Paladium					○						
Patina	○										
PT								○			

	AL	AU	BE	BO	CO	HE	HA	IT	ML	MO	VA
Palette			●								

| **Paragon** | | | | | | | | | ● | | |

	AL	AU	BE	BO	CO	HE	HA	IT	ML	MO	VA
Park Avenue					●				●		●
PA								○			

	AL	AU	BE	BO	CO	HE	HA	IT	ML	MO	VA
Patina	●										
Andover		○									○
Elegante						○					
Malibu		○									
Paladium					○						
Palatino			○		○				○		
PT								○			

	AL	AU	BE	BO	CO	HE	HA	IT	ML	MO	VA
Peignot			●						●		●
Penyoe					○						

| **Penyoe** | | | | | ● | | | | | | |
| Peignot | | ○ | | | | | | | ○ | | ○ |

	AL	AU	BE	BO	CO	HE	HA	IT	ML	MO	VA
Pepita										●	
Percepta	●										
Perpetua		○	○	○	○				○	○	
Permanent				●							
Perpetua		●	●	●	●				●	●	
Percepta	○										
Pharoah		●									
Photina										●	
Photura		●									
FU								○			
Futura	○		○	○	○	○	○		○		○
Spartan									○		
Techno		○									○
Twentieth Century									○		
Pilgrim									●		
Pioneer				●							
Piranesi				●							
Minuet							○				
PL								●			
Atlantic	○										
Plantin		○	○	○	○				○	○	○
Placard											●

AL *Alphatype*   AU *Autologic*   BE *Berthold*   BO *Bobst-Graphic*
CO *Compugraphic*   HE *Dr Hell*   HA *Harris Corporation*   IT *Itek*
ML *Mergenthaler Linotype*   MO *Monotype*   VA *Varityper*

	AL	AU	BE	BO	CO	HE	HA	IT	ML	MO	VA
Plantin		●	●	●	●				●	●	●
Atlantic	O										
PL								O			

| **PM (Paul Mark)** | | | | | | | | ● | | | |

| **Poliphilus** | | | | | | | | | | ● | |

	AL	AU	BE	BO	CO	HE	HA	IT	ML	MO	VA
Polka			●								
Ad Bold		O									
Dom					O						

| **Poppl-Pontifex** | | | ● | | | | | | | | |

	AL	AU	BE	BO	CO	HE	HA	IT	ML	MO	VA
Poster Bodoni		●							●		
Bodoni Extra Bold					O						
Ultra Bodoni											O

| **Praxis** | | | | | | ● | | | | | |

	AL	AU	BE	BO	CO	HE	HA	IT	ML	MO	VA
Premier		●									
Primer									O		
Rector	O										

Primer									●		
Premier		O									
Rector	O										

	AL	AU	BE	BO	CO	HE	HA	IT	ML	MO	VA
Primus			●								

| **Profil** | | | | ● | | | | | | | |

| **Promotor** | | ● | | | | | | | | | |

	AL	AU	BE	BO	CO	HE	HA	IT	ML	MO	VA
PT								●			
Andover		○									○
Elegante						○					
Malibu		○									
Paladium					○						
Palatino			○			○			○		
Patina	○										

	AL	AU	BE	BO	CO	HE	HA	IT	ML	MO	VA
PT Barnham											●

	AL	AU	BE	BO	CO	HE	HA	IT	ML	MO	VA
QS (Quillscript)								●			
Quill					○						

	AL	AU	BE	BO	CO	HE	HA	IT	ML	MO	VA
Quadriga Antiqua		●									

	AL	AU	BE	BO	CO	HE	HA	IT	ML	MO	VA
Quill					●						
QS							○				

	AL	AU	BE	BO	CO	HE	HA	IT	ML	MO	VA
Quorom			●		●						

	AL	AU	BE	BO	CO	HE	HA	IT	ML	MO	VA
Raphael					●						

	AL	AU	BE	BO	CO	HE	HA	IT	ML	MO	VA
Ray Shaded					●						

	AL	AU	BE	BO	CO	HE	HA	IT	ML	MO	VA
Record Gothic					●						

	AL	AU	BE	BO	CO	HE	HA	IT	ML	MO	VA
Rector	●										
Premier		○									
Primer										○	

	AL	AU	BE	BO	CO	HE	HA	IT	ML	MO	VA
Regal							●				
Aurora									○		○
Empira	○	○									○
News No 2, 12					○						
RG									○		

	AL	AU	BE	BO	CO	HE	HA	IT	ML	MO	VA
Reiter Block Reversed		●									
Repro Script											●
Revue				●							
RG								●			
Aurora									○		○
Empira	○	○									
News No 2, 12					○						
Regal							○				
Rhapsodie			●								
Riviera Script					●						
Rockwell			●	●	●					●	
Cairo							○				
Memphis			○						○		
ST								○			
Stymie	○	○			○						○
Roman					●						
Romana			●						●		
Romulus										●	
Ronaldson		●									
Ronda					●						
Rotation									●		

PHOTOCOMPOSITION TYPEFACES

	AL	AU	BE	BO	CO	HE	HA	IT	ML	MO	VA
Royal							●				
Coronna									○		
CR								○			
Crown		○									○
Koronna	○										
News No 3, 5, 6					○						
Nimbus		○									
RS							●				

	AL	AU	BE	BO	CO	HE	HA	IT	ML	MO	VA
Sabon			●						●	●	
Berner											○
Sybil		○									

	AL	AU	BE	BO	CO	HE	HA	IT	ML	MO	VA
Sans 5½/6pt					●						
Futura 5½pt							○				
Spartan									○		
Techno Book		○									○

	AL	AU	BE	BO	CO	HE	HA	IT	ML	MO	VA
Saul			●								
Continental							○				
Mediaeval											○
Olympus	○										
Trump Mediaeval		○		○	○				○		

	AL	AU	BE	BO	CO	HE	HA	IT	ML	MO	VA
Schadow Antiqua			●								

	AL	AU	BE	BO	CO	HE	HA	IT	ML	MO	VA
Schoolbook											●
Century Schoolbook	○	○	○		○	○			○	○	
Century Text		○									
Century Textbook					○						
CS								○			

AL *Alphatype*   AU *Autologic*   BE *Berthold*   BO *Bobst-Graphic*
CO *Compugraphic*   HE *Dr Hell*   HA *Harris Corporation*   IT *Itek*
ML *Mergenthaler Linotype*   MO *Monotype*   VA *Varityper*

	AL	AU	BE	BO	CO	HE	HA	IT	ML	MO	VA
Schreib-maschinenschrift		●			●						
Scotch				●					●		
Scotch Roman										●	
Script										●	
Selectra			●								
Elante					○						
Electra										○	
Seneca			●								
Serifa									●		
Serif Gothic	●	●			●				●	●	●
SG								○			
SG									●		
Serif Gothic	○	○			○				○	○	○
Signet Roundhand				●							
Simplified Arabic				●							
Sorbonne			●								
Souvenir	●	●	●	●					●	●	●
SV								○			
Souvenir Gothic		●		●							

AL *Alphatype*   AU *Autologic*   BE *Berthold*   BO *Bobst-Graphic*
CO *Compugraphic*   HE *Dr Hell*   HA *Harris Corporation*   IT *Itek*
ML *Mergenthaler Linotype*   MO *Monotype*   VA *Varityper*

PHOTOCOMPOSITION TYPEFACES

	AL	AU	BE	BO	CO	HE	HA	IT	ML	MO	VA
Spartan									●		
FU								O			
Futura	O		O	O	O	O			O		O
Photura		O									
Techno		O								O	
Twentieth Century										O	

	AL	AU	BE	BO	CO	HE	HA	IT	ML	MO	VA
Spartan									●		
Futura 5½pt						O					
Sans 5½/6pt					O						
Techno Book		O									O

	AL	AU	BE	BO	CO	HE	HA	IT	ML	MO	VA
Spectrum										●	

	AL	AU	BE	BO	CO	HE	HA	IT	ML	MO	VA
Spring		●									

	AL	AU	BE	BO	CO	HE	HA	IT	ML	MO	VA
SS (Ritascript)								●			

	AL	AU	BE	BO	CO	HE	HA	IT	ML	MO	VA
ST								●			
Cairo							O				
Memphis		O							O		
Rockwell			O	O	O					O	
Stymie	O	O			O						O

	AL	AU	BE	BO	CO	HE	HA	IT	ML	MO	VA
Standard Typewriter											●

	AL	AU	BE	BO	CO	HE	HA	IT	ML	MO	VA
Stuyvesant				●							

	AL	AU	BE	BO	CO	HE	HA	IT	ML	MO	VA
Stylon		●									

	AL	AU	BE	BO	CO	HE	HA	IT	ML	MO	VA
Stymie	●	●		●							●
Cairo							O				
Memphis		O							O		
Rockwell			O	O	O						
ST								O			

	AL	AU	BE	BO	CO	HE	HA	IT	ML	MO	VA
SV								●			
Souvenir		○	○	○	○				○	○	○
Sybil		●									
Berner											○
Sabon			○						○	○	
Symposia					●						
Syntax		●							●		
Techno		●									●
FU								○			
Futura	○		○	○	○	○	○		○		○
Photura		○									
Spartan									○		
Twentieth Century										○	
Techno Book		●									●
Futura 5½pt							○				
Sans 5½/6pt				○							
Spartan									○		
Tempo		●									
Tempora					●						
Textype									●		
Thunderbird					●						
Tiffany			●	●	●				●	●	●
TY								○			

Times

	AL	AU	BE	BO	CO	HE	HA	IT	ML	MO	VA
Times						●					
English	○										
English Times					○						
Times New 2				○							
Times New Roman			○								
Times Roman		○					○		○	○	○
TR								○			

	AL	AU	BE	BO	CO	HE	HA	IT	ML	MO	VA
Times Kyrillisch						●					

	AL	AU	BE	BO	CO	HE	HA	IT	ML	MO	VA
Times Mathematics											●
TR								○			

	AL	AU	BE	BO	CO	HE	HA	IT	ML	MO	VA
Times New 2				●							
English	○										
English Times					○						
Times						○					
Times New Roman			○								
Times Roman		○					○		○	○	○
TR								○			

	AL	AU	BE	BO	CO	HE	HA	IT	ML	MO	VA
Times New Roman			●								
English	○										
English Times					○						
Times						○					
Times New 2				○							
Times Roman		○					○		○	○	○
TR								○			

	AL	AU	BE	BO	CO	HE	HA	IT	ML	MO	VA
Times Phonetisch						●					

AL *Alphatype*   AU *Autologic*   BE *Berthold*   BO *Bobst-Graphic*
CO *Compugraphic*   HE *Dr Hell*   HA *Harris Corporation*   IT *Itek*
ML *Mergenthaler Linotype*   MO *Monotype*   VA *Varityper*

	AL	AU	BE	BO	CO	HE	HA	IT	ML	MO	VA
Times Roman		●					●		●	●	●
English	○										
English Times					○						
Times						○					
Times New 2				○							
Times New Roman			○								
TR								○			

	AL	AU	BE	BO	CO	HE	HA	IT	ML	MO	VA
TN								●			
Times New Roman		○									

	AL	AU	BE	BO	CO	HE	HA	IT	ML	MO	VA
Tom's Roman					●						

	AL	AU	BE	BO	CO	HE	HA	IT	ML	MO	VA
TR								●			
English	○										
English Times					○						
Times						○					
Times New 2				○							
Times New Roman			○								
Times Roman		○					○		○	○	○

	AL	AU	BE	BO	CO	HE	HA	IT	ML	MO	VA
Trade Gothic									●		
Alpha Gothic	○										
News Gothic		○	○		○		○			○	○

	AL	AU	BE	BO	CO	HE	HA	IT	ML	MO	VA
Trajon				●							

	AL	AU	BE	BO	CO	HE	HA	IT	ML	MO	VA
Tramp		●									
Hobo			○		○				○		

	AL	AU	BE	BO	CO	HE	HA	IT	ML	MO	VA
Trump Mediaeval			●		●	●			●		
Continental							○				
Mediaeval											○
Olympus	○										
Saul		○									

	AL	AU	BE	BO	CO	HE	HA	IT	ML	MO	VA
Twentieth Century										●	
FU								O			
Futura	O		O	O	O	O	O		O		O
Photura		O									
Spartan									O		
Techno		O									O
	AL	AU	BE	BO	CO	HE	HA	IT	ML	MO	VA
TY								●			
Tiffany			O	O	O				O	O	O
Typewriter										●	
Typewriter Large Elite					O						
	AL	AU	BE	BO	CO	HE	HA	IT	ML	MO	VA
Typewriter Large Elite			●								
Typewriter									O		
Typo				●							
	AL	AU	BE	BO	CO	HE	HA	IT	ML	MO	VA
Ulte Schwabacher			●								
Ultra Bodoni											●
Bodoni Extra Bold					O						
Poster Bodoni		O							O		
	AL	AU	BE	BO	CO	HE	HA	IT	ML	MO	VA
UN								●			
Alphavers	O										
Galaxy							O				
Univers			O	O	O	O	O		O	O	O
Uncial				●							
American Uncial		O									
	AL	AU	BE	BO	CO	HE	HA	IT	ML	MO	VA
Uncle Bill			●								
Uncle Sam					O						

	AL	AU	BE	BO	CO	HE	HA	IT	ML	MO	VA
Uncle Sam					●						
Uncle Bill			○								
Univers		●	●	●	●	●			●	●	●
Alphavers	○										
Galaxy						○					
UN							○				
University									●		
	AL	AU	BE	BO	CO	HE	HA	IT	ML	MO	VA
Uranus	●										
Ballardvale		○									
Hanover											○
Mallard					○						
ME							○				
Medallion							○				
Melior			○						○	○	
	AL	AU	BE	BO	CO	HE	HA	IT	ML	MO	VA
US								●			
Vag Rundschrift		●									
Van Dijck										●	
	AL	AU	BE	BO	CO	HE	HA	IT	ML	MO	VA
Vega							●				
Claro	○										
Geneva		○									
HE								○			
Helios					○						
Helvetica			○						○	○	
Megaron											○
Newton		○									
	AL	AU	BE	BO	CO	HE	HA	IT	ML	MO	VA
Venetian Script					●						
Lorraine		○									

	AL	AU	BE	BO	CO	HE	HA	IT	ML	MO	VA
Venture									●		
Vevey				●							

	AL	AU	BE	BO	CO	HE	HA	IT	ML	MO	VA
Walbaum			●								
Wedding Text			●		●						●
WT								○			

	AL	AU	BE	BO	CO	HE	HA	IT	ML	MO	VA
Weiss			●		●				●		
Edelweiss	○										

	AL	AU	BE	BO	CO	HE	HA	IT	ML	MO	VA
Windsor		●	●		●				●		
Winslow	○										

	AL	AU	BE	BO	CO	HE	HA	IT	ML	MO	VA
Winslow	●										
Windsor		○	○		○			○			

	AL	AU	BE	BO	CO	HE	HA	IT	ML	MO	VA
WT								●			
Wedding Text			○		○						○

	AL	AU	BE	BO	CO	HE	HA	IT	ML	MO	VA
Zapf		●	●		●				●	●	●
ZF								○			

	AL	AU	BE	BO	CO	HE	HA	IT	ML	MO	VA
Zenith						●					
Chelmsford		○									○
Musica	○										
OP							○				
Optima			○						○	○	
Optimist		○									
Oracle					○						

	AL	AU	BE	BO	CO	HE	HA	IT	ML	MO	VA
Zentenar Fraktur			●								

	AL	AU	BE	BO	CO	HE	HA	IT	ML	MO	VA
ZF								●			
Zapf		○	○		○					○	○

Part V Typefactors

The standard typefactors shown on the following pages are for use in those instances where calculations are to be based on standard letter and word spacing. Where amended spacing is to be specified then the standard typefactors shown must be modified accordingly by using program 1.

1 *to calculate a modified typefactor for plus or minus letter and word spacing*

AC		number of relative units to the em	96
×		12	12
÷		standard typefactor (from tables)	24.96
† ±		number of units letterspacing	−10
÷		1.2	1.2
M+	C	number of units wordspacing	16
÷		6	6
+	MR −		
MR	M+ C	12	12
×		number of relative units to the em	96
÷	MR =	calculator display shows the modified typefactor for minus or plus spacing	35.13

†use either the minus sign for minus letterspacing or the plus sign for plus letterspacing.

Where no typefactor has been given in the tables it can be easily calculated by using either programs 2 or 3. In 2, the higher the character count, the greater the accuracy. Program 3 should only be used as a guide when no other alternative is available.

2 *to calculate a typefactor from a given specimen of set text*

AC	typesize
÷	measure in picas
÷	column depth in lines of type
×	character count
=	calculator display shows the typefactor*

3 *to calculate a typefactor from a lower case alphabet a–z*

AC	typesize
÷	the lower case alphabet length from a–z measured in millimetres
×	120.535
=	calculator display shows the typefactor†

*resultant typefactor is for use only on setting with letter/word spacing as on specimen of set text used for calculation

†resultant typefactor is for use only on setting with letterspacing as on lc alphabet used for calculation

Abel COMPUGRAPHIC

cursive	47.50

AG ITEK

35 extra light	25.56
45 light	24.96
47 light condensed	30.59
55 medium	24.42
57 medium cond	30.18
65 bold	24.49
67 bold condensed	29.30
75 extra bold	23.49
77 extra bold cond	29.21

Akzidenz Grotesk BERTHOLD

light	25.05
light condensed	40.32
regular	24.90
super	21.93
italic	26.79
medium	25.66
medium italic	25.05
medium condensed	41.91
medium extended	19.15
bold	24.05
bold condensed	31.83
bold extended	17.49
extra bold cond ital	26.79
condensed	36.49
extended	19.59

	DR HELL
light condensed	44.28
bold condensed	45.00
extra bold cond	33.84

Akzidenz Grotesk Book BERTHOLD

ultra light	26.79
ultra light italic	25.66
light	25.81
light italic	25.66
light condensed	35.27
light condensed ital	35.27
light extended	22.88
regular	25.66
medium	23.92
medium italic	24.47
medium condensed	30.67
medium extended	20.75
bold	22.28
bold condensed	28.03
bold extended	19.33
italic	25.05
condensed	32.07
extended	21.93

	BOBST
light	27.30
light italic	27.70
regular	27.70
medium	26.20
medium italic	26.00
bold condensed	31.70
italic	27.60
condensed	35.70

Albertina MONOTYPE

roman	29.27
italic	32.33

Albion MONOTYPE

roman	27.88

Aldus
DR HELL

regular	28.08
italic	32.16

MERG LINOTYPE

regular	28.73
italic	27.18

Alpin Gothic COMPUGRAPHIC

1D regular	45.03
2D regular	40.04
2D italic	40.04

Alternate Gothic VARITYPER

No. 1	42.37
No. 2	31.99

AM ITEK

55 Medium	21.05
56 medium italic	21.10
65 bold	21.56
75 extra bold	20.37

Americana MERG LINOTYPE

regular	23.94
italic	23.94
bold	22.10
extra bold	21.39

American Antique D COMPUGRAPHIC

regular	23.70

American Classic D COMPUGRAPHIC

regular	21.90
italic	21.90
bold	20.52
extra bold	20.52

American Typewriter BERTHOLD

light	20.25
medium	20.25
bold	20.75
light condensed	27.67
medium condensed	26.96
bold condensed	26.79

COMPUGRAPHIC

light	23.31
medium	23.31
bold	23.31
light condensed	33.01
medium condensed	29.34
bold condensed	29.47
outline	24.96

MERG LINOTYPE

light	24.83
medium	23.66
bold	21.17
light condensed	32.44
medium condensed	31.43
bold condensed	30.47

MONOTYPE

light	26.00
medium	24.83
bold	23.23

entry continued on following page

light condensed	32.36
medium condensed	31.56
bold condensed	30.88

Andover VARITYPER

regular	25.18
semibold	24.77
italic	31.35

Angro DR HELL

| light | 20.28 |
| extra bold | 20.28 |

Antique COMPUGRAPHIC

| D | 23.70 |

MERG LINOTYPE

| No. 3 | 25.78 |

Antique Olive BERTHOLD

light	24.33
regular	21.82
medium	22.82
bold	21.17
italic.	23.13
condensed	29.81
compact	18.40
bold condensed	30.02
extended	17.86

BOBST

light	29.00
regular	28.50
medium	27.50

COMPUGRAPHIC

light	24.67
medium	21.92
bold	20.43
italic	22.22
medium italic	22.48
wide	17.81
nord	17.28
nord italic	19.44

MERG LINOTYPE

light	24.83
regular	22.35
bold	21.86
italic	22.85
black	21.39

Antique Open Face MERG LINOTYPE

| regular | 43.72 |

Apollo MONOTYPE

665A roman	25.52
645A roman	27.52
645A italic	28.91

Aquarius COMPUGRAPHIC

No 7	25.92
No 8	25.92
No 8 condensed	30.24

Arabic Script COMPUGRAPHIC

| light | 31.29 |
| bold | 29.37 |

Ariston BERTHOLD

regular	30.02
bold	27.14
extra	23.26

Arkona BERTHOLD

regular	31.36
medium	31.13

Armenian COMPUGRAPHIC

Aramian	15.84
Barz	15.84

Artcraft COMPUGRAPHIC

light	25.92
light italic	25.92
bold	25.92

AS ITEK

55 medium	24.31
56 medium italic	25.22
65 bold	23.35

Ascot Mediaeval BOBST

roman	30.10
small caps	27.70
italic	29.50
medium	30.40
bold	24.70

Aster COMPUGRAPHIC

regular	24.07
italic	24.30
bold	23.84

DR HELL

regular	25.28
italic	26.12
bold	25.52

MERG LINOTYPE

regular	23.94
italic	25.78
bold	23.66

Aster Latin BOBST

roman	27.40
italic	28.60
bold	25.50

AT ITEK

45 light	24.99
47 light condensed	32.47
55 medium	24.07
57 medium cond	32.03
65 bold	22.91
67 bold condensed	30.86

Augustea BERTHOLD

regular	24.61
italic	25.66
medium	25.05
bold	22.28
bold italic	23.01

Aura COMPUGRAPHIC

regular	29.52

Auriga MERG LINOTYPE

roman	24.83
italic	24.83
bold	23.94

Aurora MERG LINOTYPE

roman	22.85
No 2 bold face	22.59

VARITYPER

bold condensed	25.39

Avant Garde Gothic BERTHOLD

medium	23.92
extra light	24.05
bold	23.13
demibold	23.52
extra light oblique	25.50
medium oblique	23.92
demibold oblique	23.26
bold oblique	22.28
medium condensed	28.79
demibold cond	27.67
bold condensed	28.79
book	22.88
book oblique	25.66
book condensed	28.79

COMPUGRAPHIC

medium	23.51
extra light	24.67
bold	22.26
demibold	23.01
extra light oblique	27.03
medium oblique	23.46
demibold oblique	22.97
bold oblique	22.32
medium condensed	30.05
demibold cond	29.35
bold condensed	29.46
book	23.97
book oblique	23.96
book condensed	28.44

MERG LINOTYPE

medium	22.59
extra light	25.14
bold	22.10
demibold	22.35
medium cond	29.58
demibold cond	29.15
bold condensed	28.33
book	25.14

VARITYPER

medium	24.77
extra light	25.39

Bank Gothic MERG LINOTYPE

medium	20.11

Basilia BOBST

roman	28.90
italic	28.90
medium	29.00
medium italic	29.00

Baskerville

regular	24.61
italic	29.81
medium	23.26
bold	21.59
old face	37.08

BOBST	
regular	30.50
italic	34.20
medium	29.00
medium italic	33.30

COMPUGRAPHIC	
regular	27.82
italic	27.81
bold	26.19
bold italic	26.12
No 2 nominal	27.76
No 2 italic	32.91
No 2 bold	25.87
No 2 bold italic	29.18
italic true cut	37.08

DR HELL	
italic	30.96
bold	28.65
bold italic	27.36
light	28.89

MERG LINOTYPE	
regular	25.46
italic	29.58
bold	24.53
bold italic	27.18
No 2 nominal	26.82
No 2 italic	31.43

MONOTYPE	
regular	26.66
italic	30.72
semibold	23.24
semibold italic	23.24
bold	23.24
bold italic	23.24

VARITYPER	
regular	25.70
italic	25.71
bold	25.71

Basque

regular	53.54

Bauhaus

light	25.66
regular	25.66
medium	22.88
bold	25.66

BOBST	
light	30.20
medium	29.20

COMPUGRAPHIC	
light	28.28
medium	27.03
demi	26.63
bold	25.64
heavy	24.48

MERG LINOTYPE	
light	28.33
medium	28.33
demi	27.93
bold	26.46

BE ITEK

55 medium	31.23
56 medium italic	36.40
65 bold	26.72

Bell Gothic MERG LINOTYPE

regular	27.93
bold	27.93
black	25.78

MONOTYPE

regular	27.65
italic	29.76
bold	25.37

Bem COMPUGRAPHIC

regular	30.91
italic	34.57
bold	27.58

Bembo BERTHOLD

regular	25.66
italic	29.81
bold	23.52
bold italic	27.14

BOBST

regular	31.40
italic	35.10
bold	28.00

DR HELL

italic	34.62
extra bold	27.54
light	30.42

MERG LINOTYPE

regular	25.78
italic	29.15
bold	23.12

MONOTYPE

regular	27.70
italic	30.62
bold	25.12
bold italic	28.06

VARITYPER

regular	28.18
italic	33.21
bold	25.71
bold italic	30.87

Benguiat BERTHOLD

medium	22.16
medium italic	21.06
bold	20.25
bold italic	19.59
medium condensed	27.67
medium cond italic	25.65
bold condensed	24.47
bold cond italic	28.79
book	23.01
book italic	22.76
book condensed	28.79
book cond italic	26.96

COMPUGRAPHIC

medium	22.97
medium italic	22.16
bold	20.89
bold italic	20.59
medium condensed	29.55
medium cond italic	29.35

bold condensed	27.62
bold cond italic	27.27
book	23.41
book italic	23.31
book condensed	30.39
book cond italic	30.14
gothic medium	27.27
gothic medium italic	26.97
gothic bold	26.83
gothic bold italic	26.73
gothic heavy	26.04
gothic heavy italic	25.74
gothic book	27.37
gothic book italic	27.13

Berliner Grotesk BERTHOLD

light	28.79

Bernase Roman COMPUGRAPHIC

regular	30.63

Bernhard BERTHOLD

gothic light	31.13
gothic extra heavy	26.79
modern	28.79
modern italic	30.02
modern bold	26.79
modern bold italic	27.14
schönschrift	44.09

Berthold Script BERTHOLD

regular	33.59
medium	30.24

BG ITEK

45 light	25.34
55 medium	25.28

BH ITEK

45 light	29.05
55 medium	28.97
65 bold	25.28
75 extra bold	27.06

Binney Old Style MERG LINOTYPE

regular	23.66
italic	24.83

MONOTYPE

regular	22.89
italic	24.35

BK ITEK

55 medium	26.93
56 medium italic	32.14
65 bold	25.62
66 bold italic	31.21

BL ITEK

75 extra bold	22.19

Blado MONOTYPE

italic	36.45

Blizzard DR HELL

extra bold	35.40

BM	ITEK
45 light	23.63
46 light italic	22.56
55 medium	22.56
56 medium italic	21.97
65 bold	22.79
66 bold italic	21.51
75 extra bold	21.59
76 extra bold italic	20.41

BO	ITEK
45 light	27.22
46 light italic	26.76
55 medium	24.68
56 medium italic	28.17
65 bold	24.68
66 bold italic	26.07
67	32.01
70	28.12
85	19.91
86	20.29
87	29.45

Bodoni	BERTHOLD
regular	25.97
medium	24.61
italic	25.97
medium italic	25.97
bold italic	21.82
condensed italic	35.28
medium cond italic	30.67
bold condensed	46.47
bold cond italic	27.67
	BOBST
medium	29.40

light	31.00
light italic	31.30
	COMPUGRAPHIC
regular	27.12
italic	27.12
bold	24.75
bold italic	24.75
extra bold	19.96
extra bold italic	19.96
	DR HELL
italic	30.57
bold	27.54
bold italic	28.59
demibold	25.62
demibold italic	26.61
extra bold	22.44
extra bold italic	21.44
	MERG LINOTYPE
regular	26.82
italic	26.82
bold	26.12
bold italic	26.46
condensed	33.52
	MONOTYPE
135B regular	26.55
135B italic	28.14
504B regular	27.75
504B italic	27.23
260B bold	27.18
260B bold italic	24.55
	VARITYPER
regular	25.18
italic	25.18
bold	24.77

Bodoni Antiqua BERTHOLD

regular	25.97
medium	24.61
bold	21.27
condensed	34.99
medium condensed	31.83
bold condensed	28.79

Bodoni Book COMPUGRAPHIC

regular	29.04
italic	29.04

DR HELL

regular	29.13
italic	29.70

MERG LINOTYPE

regular	29.58
italic	30.94

VARITYPER

regular	28.31
italic	29.82

Bodoni No 2 COMPUGRAPHIC

regular /italic	30.24
bold	27.26
bold italic	27.26
extra bold	20.88
extra bold italic	20.88
bold condensed	32.99
extra bold cond	42.84

Bodoni Poster MERG LINOTYPE

regular /italic	19.53
condensed	41.90

Bolt Bold COMPUGRAPHIC

	20.16

Book COMPUGRAPHIC

regular	20.16
italic	22.68
bold	21.24
bold italic	22.32
extra bold	21.24
extra bold italic	21.96

Bookman BERTHOLD

medium	21.27
medium italic	21.33
light	23.00
light italic	22.28
demibold	21.59
demibold italic	20.16
bold	20.55
bold italic	19.59

COMPUGRAPHIC

medium	21.88
light	23.12
light italic	22.68
demibold	20.89
demibold italic	20.69
bold	20.37
bold italic	19.56

MERG LINOTYPE

regular	26.46
regular italic	26.46
medium	23.12
medium italic	22.59
light	23.94

entry continued on following page

light italic	23.12
demibold	22.10
demibold italic	22.10
bold	21.86
bold italic	20.52

	MONOTYPE
old style	26.73
old style italic	24.00

BR ITEK

| 75 extra bold | 35.22 |

Branding Iron COMPUGRAPHIC

| regular | 39.60 |

Brophy Script COMPUGRAPHIC

| regular | 39.96 |

Bruce Old Style MERG LINOTYPE

| regular | 24.83 |

	MONOTYPE
regular	25.43
italic	27.11

Brush COMPUGRAPHIC

| regular | 21.96 |

	VARITYPER
regular	31.43

Busorama COMPUGRAPHIC

light	25.20
medium	25.56
bold	24.12

Caledonia MERG LINOTYPE

regular	27.18
italic	26.82
bold	26.82
bold italic	26.82

	MONOTYPE
regular	26.24
italic	26.24
bold	26.24
bold italic	26.24

California COMPUGRAPHIC

regular	26.31
italic	26.31
bold	26.31
bold italic	27.12

Caliope Antique D COMPUGRAPHIC

| regular | 23.70 |

Calvert MONOTYPE

| light | 24.61 |
| bold | 23.80 |

Camelot COMPUGRAPHIC

regular	30.24
italic	32.76
bold	25.92
extra bold	23.76

black	21.24
condensed	38.88
condensed italic	37.80
bold condensed	29.88
extra bold cond	25.92

VARITYPER

regular	23.09
italic	23.09
bold	23.09

Candida BERTHOLD

regular	23.00
medium	22.28
italic	23.26
light condensed	40.32
medium condensed	36.81

BOBST

regular	27.50
italic	28.70
bold	28.00

COMPUGRAPHIC

regular	22.12
italic	22.22
bold	21.43

DR HELL

| light | 25.32 |
| bold | 24.30 |

MERG LINOTYPE

regular	23.94
italic	23.94
bold	23.66

MONOTYPE

regular	24.93
italic	24.77
bold	23.95

Caprice BERTHOLD

| regular | 38.84 |

Cartier COMPUGRAPHIC

| regular | 30.39 |
| italic | 40.34 |

Cascade MERG LINOTYPE

| regular | 29.15 |

Caslon Buch BERTHOLD

regular	25.97
italic	29.39
medium	25.66

Caslon Antique COMPUGRAPHIC

| regular | 34.32 |

Caslon Gotilch BERTHOLD

| regular | 28.79 |

Caslon Headline COMPUGRAPHIC

| regular | 26.88 |

Caslon Old Face No 2 MERG LINOTYPE

| regular | 29.15 |
| italic | 31.92 |

Caslon No 3 MERG LINOTYPE

| regular | 24.53 |
| italic | 26.82 |

Caslon No 76 COMPUGRAPHIC	
regular	27.12
italic	27.12

Caslon 223 COMPUGRAPHIC	
light	26.28
light italic	24.96
regular	25.56
italic	25.20
bold	25.20
bold italic	24.12
exta bold	26.64
extra bold italic	24.48

Caslon 540 MERG LINOTYPE	
regular	26.82
italic	30.47

CC ITEK	
65 bold	45.74

CD ITEK	
55 medium	26.48
56 medium italic	27.12
65 bold	25.59
66 bold italic	25.71

CE ITEK	
55 medium	26.48
56 medium italic	27.30

Celestina BOBST	
regular	28.60
italic	31.00
bold	28.60

Century BERTHOLD	
bold	26.62
ultra	19.15
ultra italic	18.33
expanded	26.62
expanded italic	25.97
COMPUGRAPHIC	
light	24.97
light italic	24.97
demibold	24.97
bold	26.28
bold italic	26.28
bold condensed	35.82
ultra	18.36
ultra italic	18.35
MERG LINOTYPE	
bold	24.53
bold italic	24.53
bold condensed	33.52
ultra	19.53
ultra italic	19.53
expanded	25.46
expanded italic	25.78
MONOTYPE	
bold	26.79
bold italic	24.10
expanded	25.71
expanded italic	27.29
VARITYPER	
expanded	23.91
expanded italic	25.39
expanded bold	21.94

Century 2 COMPUGRAPHIC

light	25.94
light italic	26.73
bold	24.41
bold italic	24.67
bold extended	21.24

Century Old Style BERTHOLD

regular	25.65
italic	28.79

COMPUGRAPHIC

regular	26.04
italic	28.16
bold	21.68

MERG LINOTYPE

regular	28.33
italic	29.58
bold	24.23

MONOTYPE

regular	28.09
italic	28.51

Century Book BERTHOLD

regular	23.52
italic	23.26

COMPUGRAPHIC

regular	24.67
italic	24.57

MERG LINOTYPE

regular	26.12
italic	25.46

Century School BOBST

regular	27.50
italic	28.30
bold	25.00
bold italic	25.90

Century Schoolbook BERTHOLD

regular	25.97
italic	25.66
bold	24.47

DR HELL

italic	26.60
light	25.64
bold	23.96

MERG LINOTYPE

regular	24.83
italic	25.14
bold	22.10

MONOTYPE

227B regular	24.50
227B italic	25.17
477 regular	21.37
477 italic	23.32
650 regular	25.71
650 italic	27.29
651 bold	23.13

Century Textbook COMPUGRAPHIC

regular	24.41
italic	24.41
bold	24.41

CH

light	27.10
light italic	27.10
regular	27.10
italic	28.20
condensed	35.00
extended	24.60
medium	26.50
medium italic	26.40
medium condensed	41.20
medium extended	22.40
bold	24.64
bold italic	23.40
bold condensed	35.10
extra bold	19.50

ITEK

light	27.48
light italic	26.98
medium	27.18
medium italic	27.11
medium condensed	31.64
bold	23.50
bold italic	25.68
bold condensed	27.70
extra bold	21.81
extra bold italic	21.68

Chelmsford

VARITYPER

regular	25.28
italic	25.28
demibold	25.28

Cheltenham

BERTHOLD

light	25.66
light italic	26.62

light condensed	34.42
bold	23.26
bold italic	24.33
bold cond italic	27.67
ultra	19.51
ultra italic	19.33
ultra condensed	25.66
ultra cond italic	25.66

COMPUGRAPHIC

light	28.51
light italic	28.61
light condensed	33.96
bold	27.36
bold italic	24.65
bold condensed	31.60
bold cond italic	29.36
bold reverse	26.64
bold reverse italic	26.64
ultra	19.65
ultra italic	19.70
ultra condensed	25.74
ultra cond italic	25.19

MERG LINOTYPE

regular	30.94
italic	32.44
bold	25.78
bold italic	25.78
ultra	21.63
ultra italic	21.39
nova	30.94
nova bold	26.12

VARITYPER

bold	26.71
bold condensed	32.34

Cheltenham Book

BERTHOLD

regular	26.62
italic	25.66
condensed	30.02

COMPUGRAPHIC

regular	26.93
italic	27.18
condensed	33.91
condensed italic	32.57

MERG LINOTYPE

regular	26.46
italic	26.46

Cheltenham Old Style

COMPUGRAPHIC

regular	32.76
italic	31.68

Chisel

COMPUGRAPHIC

regular	26.64

City

BERTHOLD

light	29.39
medium	28.60
bold	26.29

CL

ITEK

56 medium italic	31.59

Clarendon

BERTHOLD

medium	21.82
light	22.28
light condensed	32.56
bold	20.55

BOBST

regular	26.80
italic	26.90
bold	24.30

COMPUGRAPHIC

regular	21.24
condensed	29.16

DR HELL

regular	24.96
bold	22.08

MERG LINOTYPE

regular	22.85
light	22.85
bold	22.10

MONOTYPE

regular	21.86

VARITYPER

regular	21.79
italic	21.79
bold	21.79

Clarendon Book

COMPUGRAPHIC

regular	21.24
condensed	26.83

Clarinda Typewriter

MERG LINOTYPE

regular	21.17

Clearface	COMPUGRAPHIC
regular	30.14
italic	29.35
bold	29.35
bold italic	28.12
heavy	27.27
heavy italic	27.27
black	25.94
black italic	25.54

Clearface Gothic	BERTHOLD
regular	30.68
heavy	26.79
ultra bold	25.81

Cloister	COMPUGRAPHIC
regular	28.24
	MERG LINOTYPE
regular	32.97
italic	37.24
bold	29.15

CN	ITEK
45 light	22.78
55 medium	22.70
75 extra bold	21.46

CO	ITEK
45 light	29.48
55 medium	29.09
65 bold	28.71

Colonia	DR HELL
light	27.00
extra bold	22.92

Colonial	VARITYPER
regular	21.26
italic	21.41
bold	19.50
extra bold	19.38

Comenius Antiqua	BERTHOLD
regular	23.26
medium	22.28
italic	25.05
bold	19.59

Commercial Script	COMPUGRAPHIC
regular	28.37

Computer	COMPUGRAPHIC
regular	25.56
outline	25.56

Concorde	BERTHOLD
regular	25.35
italic	24.33
medium	23.26
medium italic	24.61
condensed	29.39
medium condensed	28.03
bold condensed	27.14
bold cond outline	25.66

Concorde Nova	BERTHOLD
regular	28.79
italic	28.79
medium	27.14

Condensed COMPUGRAPHIC

regular	47.88
italic	40.68

Cooper Black COMPUGRAPHIC

regular	18.72
italic	21.24
reverse	18.72

MONOTYPE

regular	21.02

VARITYPER

regular	19.50
italic	20.97

Copper COMPUGRAPHIC

regular	18.83
small	18.83

Copperplate COMPUGRAPHIC

light	16.20
heavy	16.20

Copperplate Gothic COMPUGRAPHIC

small font light	20.28
small font light cond	26.26
small font heavy	20.28
large font light	14.25
large font light cond	16.29
large font heavy	13.07

MERG LINOTYPE

29/B/C	27.93
30/B/C	27.93
31/B/C	22.10
32/B/C	22.35
33/B/C	21.39

Corona MERG LINOTYPE

regular	22.10
italic	23.66
No 2 bold	22.59

Coronet COMPUGRAPHIC

regular	38.93
bold	34.38

Corvinus BERTHOLD

regular	31.83
italic	32.30
medium	26.79
bold	23.13

CP ITEK

85 ultra bold	20.16
86 ultra bold italic	20.59
87 ultra bold cond	22.68

CR ITEK

55 medium	25.66
65 bold	25.66

Craw Modern MERG LINOTYPE

regular	24.53

Crown

Crown VARITYPER

regular	23.09
bold	23.09
condensed	23.09
bold condensed	23.09

CRT Gothic MERG LINOTYPE

light	26.46
medium	26.12
bold	23.94
black	20.95

CS ITEK

55 medium	26.47
56 medium italic	27.59
65 bold	23.66
66 bold italic	23.96
67 bold condensed	36.84

Cyrillic Gothic COMPUGRAPHIC

medium	18.29
medium italic	18.29
bold	18.29
bold italic	18.29

Cyrillic Helios II COMPUGRAPHIC

regular	13.91
italic	13.91
bold	13.91
bold italic	13.91
condensed	17.72
bold condensed	17.72

Cyrillic Impressum COMPUGRAPHIC

regular	12.87
italic	13.22
bold	12.67
bold italic	14.61

Cyrillic Times COMPUGRAPHIC

regular	18.52
bold	18.52
italic	18.97
bold italic	18.97

Deepdene VARITYPER

regular	30.57
italic	37.46
bold	28.84

Delia DR HELL

light	20.76
extra bold	20.64

Demos DR HELL

regular	25.80
bold	24.00
italic	27.96

Devinne MERG LINOTYPE

regular	25.46
italic	25.78

Didi COMPUGRAPHIC

regular	23.04

Digi-Antiqua	DR HELL
light	24.93
light condensed	23.28
bold	24.57
italic	25.14

Digi-Fraktur	DR HELL
regular	31.50

Digi-Grotesk Serie N	DR HELL
light	25.86
extra bold	24.84
extra bold cond	23.40

Digi-Grotesk Serie PTT 67	DR HELL
light	23.16
extra bold	21.24

Digi-Grotesk Serie S	DR HELL
light	28.92
bold	26.64

Digiset Colonia	BERTHOLD
light	25.66
bold	22.52

Digiset Digi-Antiqua	BERTHOLD
light	23.26
medium	23.13

Digiset Digi-Grotesk N	BERTHOLD
light	24.19
inclined	23.78
medium	23.65
light(S)	25.66
medium(S)	25.05

Digiset Folio	BERTHOLD
book	26.13
medium	26.96

Directory Gothic	COMPUGRAPHIC
regular	31.28
bold	31.28

Diskus	BERTHOLD
light	33.87
medium	30.24

Dom Casual	COMPUGRAPHIC
regular	42.99
bold	37.38
reverse	40.32

Dom Diagonal	COMPUGRAPHIC
regular	42.99
bold	37.38
reverse	40.32

Dominante BERTHOLD

regular	25.05
italic	25.97
bold	24.90
	BOBST
light	28.30
light italic	27.90
bold	27.00

Doric MERG LINOTYPE

163	30.94
black	20.73

Dutch Old Style COMPUGRAPHIC

regular	30.64
italic	33.22
bold	28.88
bold italic	31.24

Eccentric COMPUGRAPHIC

regular	33.84

Edison DR HELL

text	22.80
bold	21.78
italic	23.52
bold italic	22.44

Egizio BERTHOLD

regular	23.13
italic	24.33
bold	22.28
bold italic	21.82

	BOBST
regular	27.10
italic	27.20
bold	23.50

Egyptian COMPUGRAPHIC

bold condensed	30.24
	MERG LINOTYPE
regular	26.46
light	26.12
medium	25.78
bold	25.78
	MONOTYPE
regular	23.54

Egyptienne BERTHOLD

bold condensed	30.02

Ehrhardt BERTHOLD

regular	27.14
italic	30.90
demibold	25.05
demibold italic	28.60
	BOBST
regular	30.00
italic	32.10
medium	27.50
medium italic	31.00
	MONOTYPE
regular	27.69
italic	29.45
demibold	24.92
demibold italic	26.59
Pitman's ita	23.83
Pitman's ita demibold	21.44

Elante	COMPUGRAPHIC
regular	26.53
cursive	27.62
bold	25.74
bold cursive	26.14

Electra	MERG LINOTYPE
regular	28.73
cursive	29.15
bold	27.93

Empira	VARITYPER
regular	23.09
bold	23.09

Englische Schreibschrift	BERTHOLD
regular	30.90
medium	29.81
bold	28.03
	BOBST
regular	38.90

English Times	COMPUGRAPHIC
regular	26.76
italic	26.76
bold	26.76
bold italic	26.76

Engravers	COMPUGRAPHIC
regular	19.72
text	35.28
	MERG LINOTYPE
No 9 bold	20.73

Engravers Old English	BERTHOLD
regular	31.83
bold	25.66
	MONOTYPE
regular	29.84

Eras	BERTHOLD
light	25.05
medium	23.52
demibold	23.01
bold	21.16
ultra	20.15
	MERG LINOTYPE
light	27.93
medium	26.82
demibold	24.23
bold	21.86
ultra	21.63

Erbar	COMPUGRAPHIC
light condensed	42.48
medium condensed	42.48
	MERG LINOTYPE
light condensed	37.94
bold	22.10
bold condensed	37.24

ES	ITEK
53 extended	21.57
55 medium	24.79
73 ex bold extended	18.93
75 extra bold	23.39

Euclid	COMPUGRAPHIC
regular	22.68
bold	22.32

Eurostile	BERTHOLD
regular	23.52
italic	25.05
bold	23.01
condensed	33.59
bold condensed	31.36
extended	17.49
bold extended	17.14
	MERG LINOTYPE
regular	25.14
bold	24.55
extended	24.23
bold extended	23.66
	VARITYPER
regular	25.71
bold	21.86
extended	17.50
bold extended	16.17

EX	ITEK
55 medium	23.39
56 medium italic	22.80

Excelsior	MERG LINOTYPE
regular	22.10
italic	22.35
bold	21.39
	MONOTYPE
regular	24.35
italic	24.46
bold	23.27

Fairfield	MERG LINOTYPE
medium	27.93
medium italic	30.94

Falstaff	MONOTYPE
regular	19.23
italic	19.23

Fat Face	COMPUGRAPHIC
regular	30.60

Federal Antique D	COMPUGRAPHIC
regular	23.70

Fenice	BERTHOLD
regular	26.79
italic	26.62
bold	24.90

Figaro	MONOTYPE
regular	38.02

Firenze	COMPUGRAPHIC
regular	22.32

FL	ITEK
55	36.67

Flange	BERTHOLD
regular	21.93

Flemish Script COMPUGRAPHIC

regular	40.58
ll	43.12

Florentine Script COMPUGRAPHIC

regular	35.99
ll	37.80

Floridian Script COMPUGRAPHIC

regular	36.66

Flyer BERTHOLD

bold	22.28
bold condensed	28.79

Folio BERTHOLD

light	25.66
light italic	25.05
medium	27.49
bold	21.49
book	25.81
	DR HELL
bold	27.60
demibold	26.76
book	28.36
	MONOTYPE
light	27.49
medium	27.49
medium extended	22.15

Forte MONOTYPE

regular	27.04

Fournier MONOTYPE

regular	31.19
italic	33.16

Franklin BERTHOLD

italic	25.66
medium italic	25.66
	COMPUGRAPHIC
italic	24.42
wide	20.16
wide italic	21.24
condensed	28.08
condensed italic	28.08
extra condensed	33.84
extra cond italic	35.64

Franklin-Antiqua BERTHOLD

regular	25.05
medium	25.05
bold	23.13

Franklin Gothic BERTHOLD

regular	25.05
italic	24.47
condensed	28.03
extra condensed	32.56
	MERG LINOTYPE
regular	23.12
	VARITYPER
regular	23.27
italic	23.45
condensed	28.18
condensed italic	28.18

French Round Face MONOTYPE

regular	26.13
italic	27.73

Fritz Quadrata BERTHOLD

regular	23.52
bold	23.01

COMPUGRAPHIC

regular	24.41
bold	24.41

MERG LINOTYPE

regular	25.78
bold	24.53

Frutiger MERG LINOTYPE

55	24.53
55 italic	24.53
45 light	27.18
45 light italic	27.18
65 bold	23.94
65 bold italic	23.12
75 black	21.63
75 black italic	21.86

FU ITEK

35 extra light	32.10
36 extra light italic	33.08
45 light	31.01
46 light italic	30.70
55 medium	29.97
56 medium italic	30.19
57 medium cond	40.07
65 bold	27.53
66 bold italic	27.28

67 bold condensed	36.42
75 extra bold	24.66
76 extra bold italic	24.37
85 ultra bold	23.88
87 ultra bold cond	31.08

Futura BERTHOLD

light	27.14
light italic	29.60
light condensed	40.32
medium	27.85
medium italic	27.49
medium condensed	36.49
demibold	26.13
demibold italic	26.96
bold	22.28
bold italic	23.01
bold condensed	31.83
bold outline	21.27
extra bold	21.06
extra bold cond	26.79
ex bold cond outline	25.66

BOBST

light	32.90
light italic	33.60
light condensed	41.70
regular	32.40
italic	33.50
medium	30.20
medium italic	30.30
medium condensed	38.70
bold	25.30
bold italic	25.50
bold condensed	34.30
extra bold	23.80

extra bold cond	29.70
extra bold italic	23.70

COMPUGRAPHIC

light	29.99
light italic	29.99
medium	26.15
medium italic	26.15
medium condensed	31.87
demibold	26.15
demibold italic	26.15
bold	23.59
bold italic	23.59
bold condensed	31.86
bold cond italic	31.88
extra bold	21.60
extra bold reverse	21.60
italic reverse	21.60
bold cond reverse	31.68
bold cond ital rev	31.68

DR HELL

demibold	25.68

MERG LINOTYPE

light	25.78
bold	20.11
heavy	24.83

Futura Book BERTHOLD

regular	27.14
italic	28.79

COMPUGRAPHIC

regular	26.73
italic	26.73
condensed	31.87

DR HELL

regular	28.56

MERG LINOTYPE

regular	24.83

FZ ITEK

55 Medium	26.01
75 extra bold	24.39

Gando Ronde MERG LINOTYPE

regular	40.22

Garamond BERTHOLD

regular	28.03
italic	30.02
italic swash	29.60
light	23.13
light italic	23.00
light condensed	29.81
light cond italic	28.79
medium	25.66
medium italic	26.62
medium condensed	30.68
bold	20.55
bold italic	20.16
bold condensed	26.62
bold cond italic	25.05
ultra	19.59
ultra italic	19.15
ultra condensed	25.05
ultra cond italic	23.01

BOBST

regular	31.80
italic	35.40
174 italic	35.30
medium	28.30

entry continued on following page

regular	27.62
italic	29.60
light	25.54
light italic	25.64
light condensed	33.26
light cond italic	32.32
bold	22.67
bold italic	22.53
bold condensed	27.82
bold cond italic	28.07
ultra	21.24
ultra italic	20.79
ultra condensed	27.72
ultra cond italic	26.48

DR HELL

regular	27.72
italic	29.79
light	28.08
bold	28.08
bold italic	28.12

MERG LINOTYPE

regular	26.12
italic	26.46
bold	25.14
ultra	22.10
ultra italic	21.63

MONOTYPE

regular	27.69
italic	31.63
bold	25.68
bold italic	27.37

VARITYPER

regular	28.05
italic	28.05
bold	26.59
bold italic	26.95

Garamond Book BERTHOLD

regular	22.88
italic	22.28
condensed	28.60
condensed italic	26.62

COMPUGRAPHIC

regular	25.39
italic	25.09
condensed	31.29
condensed italic	31.48

MERG LINOTYPE

regular	26.12
italic	25.46

Garamond No 2 COMPUGRAPHIC

regular	33.12
italic	32.32
bold	29.88
bold italic	29.88

Garamond No 3 MERG LINOTYPE

regular	29.58
italic	33.52
bold	26.82
bold italic	28.73

Garamond No 49

COMPUGRAPHIC

regular	28.26
italic	28.26
bold	28.26
bold italic	28.26
extra bold	27.82
extra bold italic	27.82

Garamont

BERTHOLD

regular	27.14
italic	31.36
medium	24.47
medium italic	28.03

DR HELL

light	28.68
italic	29.48
bold	29.48

Garth Graphic

COMPUGRAPHIC

regular	25.64
italic	28.07
bold	23.02
bold italic	24.95
extra bold	22.16
condensed	32.36
bold condensed	29.35

GD

ITEK

55 medium	24.69
56 medium italic	29.14
65 bold	23.51
75 extra bold	24.21
77 extra bold cond	30.11

Geometric Light

COMPUGRAPHIC

regular	21.56
italic	21.56
demi	21.56
demi italic	21.56

Gill Sans

BERTHOLD

regular	26.96
italic	29.39
light	27.49
light italic	37.13
bold	23.92
bold italic	26.79
extra bold	20.85
ultra bold cond	27.85

BOBST

regular	30.60
italic	33.00
light	31.00
light italic	33.70
bold	27.60

COMPUGRAPHIC

medium	29.46
medium italic	31.37
light	29.80
light italic	31.68
light condensed	37.24
bold	25.25
bold condensed	30.99
ultra bold	18.36
ultra bold outline	18.36

entry continued on following page

	DR HELL
regular	27.84
light	28.20
bold	26.00
extra bold	22.64

	MERG LINOTYPE
regular	28.73
italic	30.94
light	29.58
light italic	31.42
bold	24.83
bold italic	25.46
bold condensed	26.82
extra bold.	20.95
ultra bold	18.12
condensed	40.22

	MONOTYPE
349	20.96
regular	24.96
italic	26.70
light	24.96
light italic	26.70
bold	22.87
bold italic	24.78
bold condensed	25.94
extra bold	20.55
condensed	38.88

Gill Kayo — BERTHOLD
regular	19.33

Glenn Shaded — COMPUGRAPHIC
regular	15.84

Gloucester — MONOTYPE
99 old style	29.88
99 old style italic	31.79
103 bold	26.77

GO — ITEK
55 medium	29.73
65 bold	27.19
75 extra bold	25.37

Gold Nugget — COMPUGRAPHIC
regular	14.76

Gorilla — COMPUGRAPHIC
regular	24.84

Gothic — COMPUGRAPHIC
No 1	40.32
No 2	26.64
No 3	26.64
No 4	39.24
No 5	24.48
extra light extended	21.58
outline condensed	31.68
No 4 reverse	31.32

	MERG LINOTYPE
No 13	28.33
No 16	22.85

	VARITYPER
outline caps	25.81
outline lower case	32.17

Goudy — BERTHOLD
extra bold	23.26
heavy face	20.75

bold	26.07
bold italic	24.48
bold condensed	30.89
extra bold	24.84
extra bold cond	31.27
heavy face	19.80
heavy face italic	20.88
heavy face cond	25.20
hand tooled	24.48

MERG LINOTYPE

bold	27.55
extra bold	25.46

MONOTYPE

bold	23.95
bold italic	25.24
extra bold	20.58

Goudy Catalogue BERTHOLD

regular	25.97
italic	28.03

Goudy Modern MONOTYPE

regular	29.43
italic	29.65

Goudy Old Style BERTHOLD

regular	28.03
italic	29.81

COMPUGRAPHIC

regular	28.41
italic	31.09
condensed	35.59
condensed italic	38.81

MERG LINOTYPE

regular	28.73
italic	31.43

MONOTYPE

regular	24.58
italic	26.73

Greek APLA COMPUGRAPHIC

medium	30.26
medium italic	29.35
bold	26.43
bold italic	24.85

Greek & Math COMPUGRAPHIC

regular	27.59
serif	27.59

Greek Florentine Script COMPUGRAPHIC

regular	41.40

Greek Helios II COMPUGRAPHIC

11	22.87
11 italic	22.43
11 bold	22.77
11 bold italic	22.57

Greek Oracle II COMPUGRAPHIC

regular	24.99
bold	23.56
bold italic	23.22

Greek Times COMPUGRAPHIC

regular	25.05
italic	25.39
bold	25.25
bold italic	25.19

Greek Univers II COMPUGRAPHIC

medium	25.05
medium italic	25.74
bold	23.08
bold italic	24.46

Griechisch DR HELL

italic	24.12

Griechisch Tempora DR HELL

light	23.73
demibold	23.43

Grizzly COMPUGRAPHIC

regular	26.64

Grotesk Negativ DR HELL

regular	34.02

Grotesque MONOTYPE

215 regular	24.15
215 italic	25.49
126 light	24.54
126 light italic	24.00
274 light condensed	28.29
216 bold	22.09
216 bold italic	23.95
318 condensed	31.09

Grouch COMPUGRAPHIC

regular	20.52

Hanover VARITYPER

reg/italic/demibold	23.72

Haverhill VARITYPER

reg/italic/demibold	32.34

HE ITEK

45 extra light	26.43
46 extra light italic	23.94
47 extra light cond	30.59
55 medium	24.72
56 medium italic	25.07
57 medium cond	30.39
63 bold extended	18.17
65 bold	21.69
66 bold italic	22.53
67 bold condensed	34.71
77 extra bold cond	30.39
83 ultra bold extend	14.95
85 ultra bold	20.38
86 ultra bold italic	20.27
87 ultra bold cond	25.74

Headline MONOTYPE

bold	24.34
bold italic	24.73

Helanna Script VARITYPER

regular	31.67

Heldustry COMPUGRAPHIC

regular	25.29
italic	25.29
medium	24.31
medium italic	24.31
demi	24.21
demi italic	24.21

Helios COMPUGRAPHIC

light	26.33
light italic	26.33
regular	24.33
italic	24.33
bold	24.33
bold italic	24.33
condensed	29.89
bold condensed	29.89
extra bold cond	25.86
rounded light	27.28
rounded light italic	27.62
rounded bold	25.86
rounded bold italic	26.23
rounded semibold	24.01
rounded semibold it	23.96

Helios II COMPUGRAPHIC

thin	27.10
thin italic	27.00
extra light	26.33
extra light italic	26.33
light	26.33
light italic	26.33
regular	24.19
italic	24.19
bold	24.19
bold italic	24.19
condensed	29.89
bold cond italic	29.89
bold condensed	29.89

Helvetica BERTHOLD

regular	24.90
italic	25.66
light	25.81
light italic	25.66
light condensed	31.83
light extended	21.82
medium	24.61
medium italic	24.90
medium condensed	36.49
medium extended	19.33
bold	21.93
bold italic	21.93
bold condensed	27.67
bold extended	15.79

MERG LINOTYPE

regular	26.46
italic	25.78
light	25.78
light italic	25.78
light condensed	33.52
light cond italic	33.52
thin	27.55
thin italic	27.18
bold	23.94
bold italic	24.53
bold condensed	28.73
bold outline	23.94
condensed	29.58
condensed italic	29.58

entry continued on following page

compressed	24.53
extra compressed	30.94
heavy	22.35
heavy italic	22.59
black	21.17
black italic	21.39
black condensed	28.33
black cond italic	28.33

	MONOTYPE
regular	24.99
italic	24.99
light	26.52
light italic	26.52
medium	24.99
medium italic	24.99
bold	23.80
bold condensed	26.36
bold cond italic	28.32
bold extended	23.13
condensed	32.36
compact	31.13

Heraldus   DR HELL

regular	22.62

Highland   VARITYPER

regular	25.39
italic	25.39
bold	25.39

Hobo   COMPUGRAPHIC

medium	27.92
bold	25.89
extra bold	23.76
outline	25.92

Holland Seminar   COMPUGRAPHIC

regular	32.77
italic	32.77

Holland Title   COMPUGRAPHIC

regular	36.36

Hollandese Mediaeval   COMPUGRAPHIC

regular	31.68
bold	29.52

Holsatia   DR HELL

regular	28.38
light	29.61
bold	27.48
extra bold	24.15
bold condensed	29.08
outline	27.78

Holsatia Cyrillic   DR HELL

regular	23.34
bold	22.98
extra bold cond	24.24

Honda   COMPUGRAPHIC

regular	32.40

Horley   BOBST

light	32.80
light italic	34.20
demibold	31.20
demibold italic	32.70

Horley Old Style BERTHOLD

regular	27.49
italic	31.36
bold	25.66

IB ITEK

55 medium	27.98
56 medium italic	30.71
65 bold	28.96

IC ITEK

55 medium	22.83
56 medium italic	23.12

ID ITEK

55 medium	25.06
65 bold	25.54
75 extra bold	39.96

Impressum BERTHOLD

light	22.88
light italic	24.33
medium	23.01

COMPUGRAPHIC

regular	23.16
italic	23.94
bold	22.84
bold italic	22.38

DR HELL

italic	24.08
light	23.44
bold	23.61
bold italic	23.08

Imprint BERTHOLD

regular	25.97
italic	28.79
bold	23.13
bold italic	24.61

MERG LINOTYPE

regular	26.82
bold	23.66

MONOTYPE

regular	25.45
italic	26.92
bold	22.71
bold italic	23.04

Impuls BERTHOLD

regular	32.07

Inflex MONOTYPE

bold	20.44

Ionic BOBST

regular	24.90
italic	25.50
bold	25.30

MERG LINOTYPE

regular	22.12
italic	22.10
bold	21.39

MONOTYPE

regular	21.42
italic	22.89

Iridium MERG LINOTYPE

regular	24.83
italic	25.14
bold	24.53

Isabella COMPUGRAPHIC

regular	35.18

Italia BERTHOLD

book	25.97
medium	25.66
bold	25.05
	COMPUGRAPHIC
book	25.94
medium	25.64
bold	25.74

Italian Old Style BERTHOLD

regular	27.14
italic	29.60
bold	25.97

JA ITEK

55 medium	27.06
56 medium italic	29.48

Janson MERG LINOTYPE

regular	26.82
italic	30.47
	VARITYPER
regular	26.14
italic	28.58

Kabel BERTHOLD

medium	24.47
demi	24.47
bold	23.92
ultra	24.61
book	25.05
	COMPUGRAPHIC
medium	24.99
demi	25.08
bold	24.85
ultra	24.37
book	26.83
	MERG LINOTYPE
medium	27.55
bold	25.78
ultra	25.46
book	27.55

Kapitellia DR HELL

extra bold	26.52

Kaylin Script VARITYPER

regular	35.93

Kennerley COMPUGRAPHIC

italic	31.26
bold	24.66
bold italic	26.23
old style	29.06

KL ITEK

45 extra light	28.46
55 medium	26.98
65 bold	26.47

| 75 extra bold | 26.09 |
| 85 ultra bold | 25.58 |

Klang MONOTYPE

| regular | 27.56 |

KN ITEK

45 extra light	27.86
55 medium	27.03
65 bold	24.82
75 ultra bold	22.16

Korinna BERTHOLD

regular	25.19
italic	24.47
bold	25.05
bold italic	23.52
extra bold	22.28
extra bold italic	23.01
heavy	20.55
heavy italic	21.93
outline	22.28

BOBST

| regular | 29.80 |
| bold | 27.70 |

COMPUGRAPHIC

regular	24.98
bold	24.47
extra bold	22.43
heavy	20.10
outline	22.68

MERG LINOTYPE

| regular | 27.55 |
| bold | 26.82 |

| extra bold | 24.23 |
| heavy | 21.63 |

VARITYPER

| regular | 27.80 |
| bold | 27.18 |

Korinna Kursiv COMPUGRAPHIC

regular	25.74
bold	23.46
extra bold	22.18
heavy	20.59

Latin COMPUGRAPHIC

| extra condensed | 41.04 |

LE ITEK

55 medium	27.27
56 medium italic	27.78
65 bold	27.23
77 extra bold cond	27.19

LG ITEK

35 extra light	23.29
45 light	24.07
55 medium	22.23
65 bold	22.78
75 extra bold	23.12

Liberty COMPUGRAPHIC

| regular | 39.80 |

Libra COMPUGRAPHIC

| regular | 26.64 |

Life	BERTHOLD
light	25.97
italic	26.79
bold	25.66

Lightline Gothic	BERTHOLD
regular	29.81

Linoscript	MERG LINOTYPE
regular	41.90

Linotext	MERG LINOTYPE
regular	30.47

Lisbon	COMPUGRAPHIC
regular	30.96
italic	30.96
cursive	35.28
bold	28.80
bold italic	28.80

London Text	BERTHOLD
regular	24.61
	COMPUGRAPHIC
regular	44.70

Lubalin Graph	BERTHOLD
regular	21.16
light	21.27
medium	22.28
bold	21.93

	COMPUGRAPHIC
regular	23.04
medium	21.60
bold	22.32
	MERG LINOTYPE
extra light	22.85
medium	21.86
demi	22.59
bold	22.59

Luce	BOBST
regular	31.30
italic	31.70

Machine	COMPUGRAPHIC
regular	25.92
bold	27.00

Madison	BERTHOLD
regular	25.66
medium	23.26
bold	19.33
condensed	30.24
medium condensed	27.85

Mallard	COMPUGRAPHIC
regular	25.47
italic	25.71
bold	24.97

Mallard II	COMPUGRAPHIC
regular	25.19
italic	26.04
bold	24.31
bold italic	25.19

Manhattan COMPUGRAPHIC

regular	23.40

Marconi DR HELL

text	24.42
italic	25.44
bold	22.38
bold italic	22.92

McCullough COMPUGRAPHIC

regular	33.48

MD ITEK

55 medium	26.16
56 medium italic	30.49
65 bold	24.87
75 extra bold	22.78

ME ITEK

55 medium	25.33
56 medium italic	25.54
65 bold	24.12

Media BOBST

regular	28.30
italic	29.20
condensed	32.40
medium	28.10
medium condensed	32.30
bold	28.00

Medici MERG LINOTYPE

regular	32.97

Megaron VARITYPER

light	26.83
light italic	26.83
medium	24.57
medium italic	24.57
medium condensed	25.71
medium cond italic	25.71
bold	25.57
bold italic	24.57
bold condensed	28.71
extra bold	20.08
extra bold cond	22.50
medium extra cond	36.14

Melior BERTHOLD

regular	24.67
italic	25.05
bold	23.26

	MERG LINOTYPE
regular	24.53
italic	24.53
bold	24.23
bold italic	23.66

	MONOTYPE
regular	26.63
italic	27.55
semibold	25.96

Memphis BERTHOLD

extra light	24.90
light	25.05
medium	25.05
bold	22.28

entry continued on following page

	MERG LINOTYPE
light	24.83
light italic	24.53
medium	23.94
medium italic	24.23
bold	23.94
bold italic	23.94
extra bold	20.11
extra bold italic	20.11
medium condensed	30.47
bold condensed	30.01
extra bold cond	29.57

Meridien
	MERG LINOTYPE
regular	25.46
italic	28.73
medium	24.53
bold	22.35

Metrolite No 2
	MERG LINOTYPE
regular	26.46
italic	26.46

Metromedium No 2
	MERG LINOTYPE
regular	28.33
italic	28.73

Metroblack No 2
	MERG LINOTYPE
regular	25.46
italic	25.78

Microstyle
	COMPUGRAPHIC
regular	26.84
bold	23.39
extended	23.39
bold extended	21.51

Milano Roman
	COMPUGRAPHIC
regular	22.68

Mique
	COMPUGRAPHIC
regular	25.13

Modern
	MERG LINOTYPE
regular	22.59
	MONOTYPE
regular	26.79
italic	28.51
extended	25.71
extended italic	27.39
bold	26.35
bold italic	27.39
condensed	30.09
condensed italic	32.06

Modern Blackletter
	COMPUGRAPHIC
regular	31.09

Monanti
	DR HELL
regular	18.24
bold	18.24

Monoline Script
	MONOTYPE
italic	29.61

Monotype Grotesque MERG LINOTYPE

regular	25.46
italic	26.12
light	26.82
light italic	27.18
bold	23.12
bold italic	23.39

Monticello MERG LINOTYPE

regular	26.82
italic	28.73

Morges BOBST

regular	28.40
italic	29.20
bold	27.10

Murray COMPUGRAPHIC

regular	40.05
bold	35.59

Murray Hill BERTHOLD

regular	34.69

Napoleon DR HELL

regular	24.42
light	25.44
bold	22.74
extra bold	21.18
extra bold cond	24.24
outline	20.52

Neo Didot MONOTYPE

regular	27.32
italic	28.93

Neon COMPUGRAPHIC

regular	20.16

Neuzit BERTHOLD

bold	25.05
book	26.79

MERG LINOTYPE

regular	22.10
bold condensed	36.57
black	23.12
black condensed	15.12

MONOTYPE

regular	26.66
bold	25.04

New Bostonian COMPUGRAPHIC

regular	29.79

New Clarendon MONOTYPE

regular	23.19
bold	20.89

News No 2 TTS COMPUGRAPHIC

regular	23.15
italic	23.15
bold	23.15

News No 3, 4, 5, 6 TTS COMPUGRAPHIC

italic	23.15
bold	23.15

News No 8 TTS COMPUGRAPHIC

regular	22.32

News No 9 TTS COMPUGRAPHIC

regular	23.15
bold	23.15

News No 10 TTS COMPUGRAPHIC

regular	24.62
bold	24.62

News No 12 TTS COMPUGRAPHIC

regular	23.15
italic	23.15
bold	23.15

News No 14 TTS COMPUGRAPHIC

regular	21.66
italic	21.66
bold	21.66

News Gothic BERTHOLD

regular	30.02
bold	26.79

COMPUGRAPHIC

regular	25.77
bold	25.77
condensed	34.46
bold condensed	34.46
light	27.36
light italic	27.36
No 2 condensed	31.38
No 2 bold cond	30.86
No 3 condensed	26.28
No 3 bold cond	26.16
No 49 regular	26.01
No 49 bold	26.01

MONOTYPE

regular	24.20
italic	25.60
bold	23.95
condensed	30.56
bold condensed	28.23

VARITYPER

regular	24.97
bold	24.97
condensed	30.57
bold condensed	29.54
condensed italic	30.57

News Plantin MONOTYPE

regular	27.49
italic	28.58
bold	26.18
bold italic	26.54

Newtext BERTHOLD

regular	18.73
italic	19.59
light	19.07
light italic	19.51
demi	18.65
demi italic	19.51

COMPUGRAPHIC

regular	23.56

italic	23.96
light	24.11
light italic	24.61
demi	23.32
demi italic	23.72

MERG LINOTYPE

regular	22.85
italic	23.12
light	23.39
light italic	23.66
demi	22.85
demi italic	23.12

Newtext Book　BERTHOLD

regular	19.33
italic	19.51

COMPUGRAPHIC

regular	23.81
italic	24.31

MERG LINOTYPE

regular	23.12
italic	23.66

NG　ITEK

55 medium	28.16
57 medium cond	34.86
65 bold	25.05
67 bold condensed	34.37

Nikis　DR HELL

light	26.60
italic	30.16
bold	25.56
bold italic	28.08

Nork　COMPUGRAPHIC

light	17.43
light italic	17.43
bold	17.43

Novarese　COMPUGRAPHIC

medium	26.73
medium italic	33.02
bold	24.95
bold italic	28.81
ultra	22.08

Novarese Book　COMPUGRAPHIC

regular	27.08
italic	34.12

Novelta　BOBST

regular	30.00
bold	29.60

NT　ITEK

45 light	23.25
46 light italic	23.75
65 bold	23.02
66 bold italic	23.45

Number 21　MERG LINOTYPE

regular	24.53

Nuptial　MERG LINOTYPE

regular	37.24

Nyon	BOBST
regular	31.50
italic	32.30
bold	30.30

OCR-B	DR HELL
regular	21.84

Octavian	MONOTYPE
regular	31.13
italic	31.39

Old English	COMPUGRAPHIC
regular	28.77

Old English Text	MONOTYPE
regular	29.02

Old Style	MERG LINOTYPE
No 2 regular	25.22
No 2 italic	26.90
No 7 regular	26.46
No 7 italic	27.55
53 bold	23.29
53 bold italic	23.29
544 bold	25.85
	MONOTYPE
regular	26.24
italic	27.83
544 bold	26.79
53 bold	23.80
bold italic	23.85

Olympia	DR HELL
light	22.20
bold	22.20

Olympian	MERG LINOTYPE
regular	22.85
italic	23.39
bold	22.85

OP	ITEK
45 light	25.20
46 light italic	25.48
55 medium	24.64
56 medium italic	25.38
65 bold	17.44
66 bold italic	25.76

Optima	BERTHOLD
regular	24.61
italic	25.05
bold	25.05
	MERG LINOTYPE
regular	26.46
italic	26.82
medium	24.83
medium italic	24.83
bold	26.12
bold italic	26.12
black	24.83
black italic	24.83
	MONOTYPE
regular	27.93
italic	28.73
semibold	27.71

Oracle COMPUGRAPHIC

regular	26.00
italic	26.00
bold	26.00

Oracle II COMPUGRAPHIC

regular	26.63
italic	27.13
bold	25.94
bold italic	26.04

Original Script COMPUGRAPHIC

regular	41.08

Orion MERG LINOTYPE

regular	26.12
italic	26.12

PA ITEK

56	38.25

Pabst MERG LINOTYPE

extra bold	20.52
extra bold italic	20.11

Packard COMPUGRAPHIC

regular	31.71
bold	31.71

Paladium COMPUGRAPHIC

regular	26.64
italic	26.64
semibold	26.64

Palatino BERTHOLD

regular	26.62
italic	30.90
bold	26.79

DR HELL

italic	32.64
bold	28.32

MERG LINOTYPE

regular	24.83
italic	28.33
bold	24.23
bold italic	25.46

Palette BERTHOLD

regular	29.81

Paragon MERG LINOTYPE

regular	22.59
No 2 bold face	23.12

Park Avenue COMPUGRAPHIC

regular	34.39

MERG LINOTYPE

regular	36.57

VARITYPER

regular	32.68

Penyoe COMPUGRAPHIC

bold	27.34

Pepita MONOTYPE

italic	32.82

Permanent BOBST

light	29.50
light italic	29.30
medium	28.50

Perpetua BERTHOLD

regular	25.66
italic	29.60
bold	22.88
bold italic	24.61
black	21.27

BOBST

regular	32.50
italic	33.80
bold	27.30

COMPUGRAPHIC

bold	28.08

MERG LINOTYPE

regular	30.94
italic	37.95
bold	27.18
bold italic	31.92

MONOTYPE

regular	29.85
italic	33.33
bold	25.82

Photina MONOTYPE

regular	25.73
italic	27.55
semi-bold	25.67

Pilgrim MERG LINOTYPE

regular	24.53
italic	24.53

Pioneer COMPUGRAPHIC

regular	20.52

Piranesi COMPUGRAPHIC

italic	39.44

PL ITEK

45 light	27.61
55 medium	27.61
56 medium italic	28.50
65 bold	24.01

Placard MONOTYPE

condensed	37.88
bold condensed	30.28

Plantin BERTHOLD

regular	25.97
italic	29.60
bold	24.47
bold italic	24.47

BOBST

regular	29.60
italic	30.40
bold	26.30
bold italic	25.50

COMPUGRAPHIC

regular	28.47
italic	30.43
bold	25.28
bold italic	25.13

	MERG LINOTYPE
regular	26.82
italic	29.15
bold	26.46
bold italic	26.12

	MONOTYPE
regular	25.45
italic	26.92
light	25.45
light italic	26.92
semibold	23.15
semibold italic	22.94
bold	22.63
bold italic	22.42

PM ITEK

75 extra bold	25.56

Poliphilus MONOTYPE

regular	31.97
italic	36.45

Poppl-Pontifex BERTHOLD

regular	23.26
italic	25.05
medium	22.28

Praxis DR HELL

regular	27.72
extra bold	25.56

Primer MERG LINOTYPE

regular	25.46
italic	25.78

Primus BERTHOLD

light italic	23.26

Primus Antiqua BERTHOLD

light	23.26
medium	23.52

Profil COMPUGRAPHIC

regular	13.68

Promoter BERTHOLD

regular	16.86

PT ITEK

55 medium	26.30
56 medium italic	29.95
65 bold	25.88
66 bold italic	26.30

PT Barnum VARITYPER

regular	27.07

QS ITEK

56 medium italic	39.22

Quadriga Antiqua BERTHOLD

regular	26.62
demibold	25.66
bold	24.61
extra bold	23.13

Quill COMPUGRAPHIC

regular	43.56

Quorum	BERTHOLD
light	27.67
book	26.96
medium	25.05
bold	25.05
black	25.05
	COMPUGRAPHIC
light	26.18
book	24.85
medium	24.95
bold	25.09
black	23.88

Raphael	COMPUGRAPHIC
regular	28.44

Ray Shaded	COMPUGRAPHIC
regular	15.84

Record Gothic	COMPUGRAPHIC
bold italic	28.44
condensed italic	37.08

Repro Script	VARITYPER
regular	47.63

Revue	COMPUGRAPHIC
regular	24.48

RG	ITEK
55 medium	24.04
65 bold	23.28

Rhapsodie	BERTHOLD
regular	24.47

Riviera Script	COMPUGRAPHIC
regular	42.87

Rockwell	BERTHOLD
regular	24.47
italic	24.47
light	24.90
light italic	24.05
bold	22.28
bold italic	23.52
extra bold	19.59
condensed	39.56
bold condensed	31.36
	BOBST
regular	28.00
italic	27.80
light	28.70
light italic	28.20
bold	26.80
	COMPUGRAPHIC
medium	23.72
medium italic	23.42
light	24.01
light italic	24.21
bold	22.97
bold italic	23.22
extra bold	18.51
medium condensed	37.73
bold condensed	29.94

	MONOTYPE
regular	23.93
italic	23.93
light	23.93
light italic	23.93
bold	22.35
bold italic	22.35
extra bold	19.26
condensed	34.76

Roman COMPUGRAPHIC

shaded	39.93
stylus	39.97

Romana BERTHOLD

ultra	25.97

MERG LINOTYPE

bold	25.46
extra bold	25.14

Romulus MONOTYPE

regular	29.62
italic	28.82
bold	28.08
bold italic	27.74

Ronda COMPUGRAPHIC

regular	26.64
light	26.64
bold	26.28

Rotation MERG LINOTYPE

regular	25.78
italic	25.46
bold	25.78

RS ITEK

56 medium italic	31.65

Sabon BERTHOLD

italic	26.79

MERG LINOTYPE

regular	26.12
italic	26.12
bold	26.12

MONOTYPE

regular	27.41
italic	27.41
semibold	27.41

Sabon Antiqua BERTHOLD

regular	27.85
medium	27.14

Sans COMPUGRAPHIC

No 1 TTS regular	23.18
No 1 TTS heavy	23.18
No 2 TTS regular	23.15
No 2 TTS heavy	23.15
No 3 TTS regular	22.32

Schadow Antiqua BERTHOLD

light	24.61
medium	23.01
bold	20.55
bold condensed	32.56

Schoolbook VARITYPER

regular	23.36
italic	23.36
bold	20.83
bold italic	20.83

Schreib-machinenschrift BERTHOLD

regular	16.86

DR HELL

regular	20.64

Scotch COMPUGRAPHIC

regular	25.92
italic	25.92

MERG LINOTYPE

regular	26.46
italic	28.73

Scotch Roman MONOTYPE

regular	24.75
italic	26.28

Script MONOTYPE

italic	28.94

Seneca BERTHOLD

regular	28.03
italic	28.03
medium	26.62
bold	24.61
extra bold	22.88

Serifa MERG LINOTYPE

55 regular	23.94
65 bold	22.85
56 italic	24.23
75 extra bold	21.63

Serif Gothic BERTHOLD

regular	25.05
light	25.05
bold	26.79
extra bold	27.14
heavy	25.66
black	25.05
outline	24.47

COMPUGRAPHIC

regular	25.97
light	26.38
bold	25.97
extra bold	25.20
heavy	24.84
black	23.42
outline	30.60

MERG LINOTYPE

regular	25.78
light	27.18
bold	25.78
extra bold	25.78
heavy	25.14

MONOTYPE

regular	27.29
light	28.51
bold	27.29
extra bold	27.43
heavy	26.36
black	27.04

COPYFITTING TYPEFACTORS

	VARITYPER
regular	26.26
bold	26.03

SG	ITEK
45 light	27.74
55 medium	26.17
65 bold	26.09
75 extra bold	26.17
85 ultra bold	25.28

Signet Roundhand	COMPUGRAPHIC
regular	32.57

Simplified Arabic	COMPUGRAPHIC
regular	28.86
light	28.86
bold	26.93

Sorbonne	BERTHOLD
regular	26.79
italic	29.39
medium	26.62
bold	26.79
medium condensed	32.56

Souvenir	BERTHOLD
light	26.62
light italic	26.62
medium	25.66
medium italic	25.05
demibold	23.13
demibold italic	23.26

bold	21.93
bold italic	21.27

	BOBST
light	30.00
light italic	30.00
medium	27.70
medium italic	28.00
bold	23.90

	COMPUGRAPHIC
light	27.99
light italic	27.99
medium	26.28
medium italic	26.28
demibold	24.32
demibold italic	24.32
bold	22.71
bold italic	22.71

	MERG LINOTYPE
light	27.55
light italic	27.55
medium	25.78
medium italic	25.78
demibold	23.94
demibold italic	23.94
bold	22.35
bold italic	22.10
bold outline	22.35

	MONOTYPE
light	27.85
light italic	27.85
medium	26.48
medium italic	26.48
demibold	24.43

entry continued on following page

demibold italic	24.43
bold	23.13
bold italic	23.13

VARITYPER

regular	26.83
italic	26.59
demibold	24.09
demibold italic	23.91

Souvenir Gothic BERTHOLD

light	29.81
light italic	29.81
medium	26.79
medium italic	26.96
demibold	25.66
demibold italic	25.66

COMPUGRAPHIC

light	29.80
light italic	29.40
medium	26.28
medium italic	26.53
demibold	24.95
demibold italic	25.19

Spartan MERG LINOTYPE

light	30.94
light italic	30.94
book	26.82
book italic	29.15
book condensed	32.44
medium	30.47
medium italic	30.94
medium condensed	31.43
bold	26.82
bold italic	26.82

bold condensed	35.28
heavy	26.46
heavy italic	26.46
heavy condensed	30.94
black	23.39
black italic	23.39
black condensed	30.94
black cond italic	31.43
extra black	20.11
extra black italic	20.32
extra black cond	25.14

Spectrum MONOTYPE

regular	30.26
italic	38.36
semibold	33.32

SS ITEK

56 medium italic	31.64

ST ITEK

45 light	26.47
55 medium	26.93
56 medium italic	26.76
65 bold	23.46
66 bold italic	24.25
85 ultra bold	22.00
86 ultra bold italic	21.85
87 ultra bold cond	32.99

Standard Typewriter VARITYPER

regular	21.48

Stuyvesant COMPUGRAPHIC

regular	42.71

Stymie COMPUGRAPHIC

light	26.04
light italic	25.93
medium	25.82
medium italic	25.82
bold	24.31
bold italic	24.31
extra bold	25.20
extra bold cond	31.32
hairline	26.64

VARITYPER

light	24.97
light italic	24.97
medium	22.75
medium italic	22.75

SV ITEK

45 light	26.47
46 light italic	27.03
55 medium	24.86
56 medium italic	24.70
65 bold	23.19
66 bold italic	22.97
75 extra bold	21.33
76 extra bold italic	20.58

Symposia COMPUGRAPHIC

regular	26.76
italic	26.76
bold	26.76

Syntax BERTHOLD

regular	26.79
italic	26.79
medium	26.62
extra bold	20.55

MERG LINOTYPE

regular	26.46
bold	26.12
black	21.39

Techno VARITYPER

medium	28.98
medium italic	28.98
bold	26.83
bold italic	26.83
extra bold	23.36

Tempora DR HELL

light	26.80
italic	26.96
semibold	25.40

Textype MERG LINOTYPE

regular	27.93
italic	29.58
bold	23.12
bold italic	22.85

Thunderbird COMPUGRAPHIC

extra condensed	46.44

Tiffany

light	24.61
medium	22.64
demibold	21.93
bold	18.33

BOBST

light	27.60
bold	25.70

COMPUGRAPHIC

light	26.18
medium	24.12
demibold	24.12
heavy	20.45

MERG LINOTYPE

light	25.46
medium	23.94
demibold	23.94
heavy	20.31

MONOTYPE

light	26.91
medium	25.60
demibold	25.43
heavy	21.82

VARITYPER

medium	24.38
heavy	20.41

Times

DR HELL

italic	28.26
light	27.12
extra bold	27.54
extra bold italic	29.19

Times New Roman

BERTHOLD

roman	25.97
italic	27.14
bold	27.14
bold italic	25.97
extra bold	23.92

Times Roman

MERG LINOTYPE

roman	28.33
italic	29.15
semibold	26.82
semibold italic	27.93
bold	26.46
bold italic	27.93

MONOTYPE

roman	25.82
italic	26.89
semibold	24.48
semibold italic	25.61
bold	26.89
bold italic	26.89
bold condensed	30.68
condensed	30.18
condensed italic	32.69

VARITYPER

roman	26.83
italic	26.83
bold	26.83
bold italic	26.83

Times New 2 BOBST

roman	28.40
italic	28.50
bold	28.50
bold italic	28.50

Times Kyrillisch DR HELL

light	23.46
extra bold	23.40

Times Mathematics MONOTYPE

regular	26.98
italic	28.03
bold	27.76
bold italic	26.42

TN ITEK

55 medium	25.82

Tom's Roman COMPUGRAPHIC

regular	25.15

TR ITEK

50 medium pi font	27.59
51 medium pi font sc	27.59
55 medium	27.59
56 medium italic	26.95
65 bold	25.69
66 bold italic	25.56
75 extra bold	25.92
76 extra bold italic	25.88

Trade Gothic MERG LINOTYPE

regular	27.18
italic	27.18
light	27.55
light italic	27.55
bold	28.33
No 2 bold	27.18
No 2 bold italic	27.18
No 18 condensed	33.52
No 18 cond italic	33.52
No 20 bold cond	31.92
No 20 bold cond ital	31.92
No 17 extra cond	41.05
No 19 bold ext cond	36.57
No 19 extended	20.95
No 19 bold extend	20.73

Trajon BOBST

regular	30.60
italic	30.50
bold	30.30

Trump Mediaeval BERTHOLD

regular	24.05
italic	23.26
bold	23.26
extra bold	19.15

COMPUGRAPHIC

regular	25.05
italic	25.05
bold	25.05
bold condensed	31.34
condensed	31.34
condensed italic	31.14

entry continued on following page

	DR HELL
regular	27.96
italic	28.80
bold	28.44
	MERG LINOTYPE
regular	23.66
italic	23.94
bold	24.53
bold italic	23.66

Twentieth Century

	MONOTYPE
light	29.77
light italic	31.39
medium	28.80
medium italic	29.84
bold	27.29
bold italic	30.00

TY

	ITEK
45 light	25.71
55 medium	24.36
65 bold	24.30
75 extra bold	20.50

Typewriter COMPUGRAPHIC

large elite	26.28
	MONOTYPE
justified	21.33
58 unit fixed space	19.86

Typo COMPUGRAPHIC

roman	38.52
upright	41.58

Ulte Schwabacher BERTHOLD

regular	28.60

Ultra Bodoni VARITYPER

regular	18.67
italic	18.62

UN ITEK

45 light	31.04
46 light italic	30.78
47 light condensed	41.08
48 light cond italic	40.10
53 medium extend	24.12
55 medium	28.23
56 medium italic	28.30
57 medium cond	39.93
58 medium cond ital	38.59
63 bold extended	22.57
65 bold	27.53
66 bold italic	27.17
67 bold condensed	34.57
68 bold cond ital	34.97
73 ex bold extended	20.89
75 extra bold	24.65
76 extra bold italic	25.44
83 ultra bold extend	20.57

Uncial COMPUGRAPHIC

regular	20.11

Uncle Sam COMPUGRAPHIC

regular	16.92
open	16.92
stars/stripes	16.92

Univers

39 ult light ext cond	53.59
45 light	26.13
46 light italic	25.19
47 light condensed	36.81
48 light cond italic	34.69
49 extra light cond	53.58
53 medium expand	20.75
55 medium	24.61
56 medium italic	25.05
57 medium cond	31.36
58 med cond italic	30.68
59 extra condensed	41.10
63 bold expanded	19.33
65 bold	23.13
66 bold italic	23.13
67 bold condensed	29.39
68 bold cond italic	29.39
73 extra bold exp	19.15
75 extra bold	22.28
76 extra bold italic	22.28
83 ultra bold exp	18.40
85 ultra bold	22.28

45 light	27.60
46 light italic	27.30
47 light condensed	40.30
53 medium expand	23.40
55 medium	27.30
56 medium italic	28.30
57 medium cond	35.80
58 med cond italic	35.70
59 extra condensed	41.70
63 bold expanded	22.30
65 bold	26.10
66 bold italic	25.80

67 bold condensed	31.90
73 extra bold exp	21.10
75 extra bold	24.70
76 extra bold italic	23.80

45 light	27.00
46 light italic	27.00
47 light condensed	37.66
48 light cond italic	37.68
49 extra light cond	62.60
53 medium expand	22.67
55 medium	27.00
56 medium italic	27.00
57 medium cond	37.68
58 med cond italic	37.65
59 extra condensed	45.15
63 bold expanded	20.81
65 bold	24.00
66 bold italic	24.00
67 bold condensed	34.63
68 bold cond italic	34.63
73 extra bold exp	20.81
75 extra bold	24.00
76 extra bold italic	24.00
83 ultra bold exp	19.06

45 light	26.12
46 light italic	26.12
47 light condensed	32.44
48 light cond italic	32.44
49 extra light cond	36.57
53 medium expand	26.12
55 medium	24.23
56 medium italic	24.23

entry continued on following page

57 medium cond	29.15
58 med cond italic	28.73
63 bold expanded	24.83
65 bold	23.66
66 bold italic	23.66
67 bold condensed	27.93
68 bold cond italic	27.93
73 extra bold exp	23.66
75 extra bold	21.39
76 extra bold italic	21.39

MONOTYPE

39 ult light ext cond	58.84
45 light	24.63
46 light italic	24.63
47 light condensed	33.25
48 light cond italic	33.25
49 extra light cond	53.29
53 medium expand	19.38
55 medium	24.70
56 medium italic	24.70
57 medium cond	30.54
58 med cond italic	30.54
59 extra condensed	40.46
63 bold expanded	19.38
65 bold	21.74
66 bold italic	21.74
67 bold condensed	28.06
68 bold cond italic	28.06
73 extra bold exp	17.86
75 extra bold	21.66
76 extra bold italic	21.66

VARITYPER

45 light	24.97
46 light italic	24.97
55 medium	25.59
56 medium italic	25.59

65 bold	23.99
66 bold italic	23.99
75 extra bold	21.79

Univers 11   COMPUGRAPHIC

light	26.84
light italic	26.84
medium	25.22
medium italic	25.22
medium expanded	21.94
medium condensed	34.78
medium cond italic	34.78
bold	25.22
bold italic	25.22
bold expanded	20.72
bold condensed	31.22
bold cond italic	31.22
ultra bold expanded	18.53

Univers
Large Face   DR HELL

45 light	28.20
47 light condensed	39.76
55 medium	26.79
57 medium cond	35.26
65 bold	31.29
67 bold condensed	33.96
75 extra bold	23.85
85 ultra bold	19.38

Univers
Small Face   DR HELL

45 light	32.52
55 medium	31.48
65 bold	28.52
75 extra bold	26.52

Univers Phonetisch	DR HELL
55 medium	31.48

University	MERG LINOTYPE
regular	32.97
italic	32.44

US	ITEK
55 medium	25.88
56 medium italic	25.45
65 bold	23.74
75 extra bold	21.00

Vag Rundschrift	BERTHOLD
regular	23.13

Van Dijck	MONOTYPE
regular	30.72
italic	35.12

Venetian Script	COMPUGRAPHIC
regular	39.95
11	42.48

Venture	MERG LINOTYPE
regular	30.02

Vevey	BOBST
regular	30.60
italic	34.00
bold	29.40

Walbaum Book	BERTHOLD
regular	24.47
italic	24.33
medium	21.93
medium italic	23.00
bold	21.82
bold italic	21.82

Walbaum Fraktur	BERTHOLD
regular	30.90

Walbaum Standard	BERTHOLD
regular	24.61
italic	25.66

Wedding Text	COMPUGRAPHIC
regular	37.52
	VARITYPER
regular	30.72

Weiss	COMPUGRAPHIC
regular	28.48
italic	34.57
bold	27.92
extra bold	26.18

Weiss Antiqua BERTHOLD

regular	28.03
italic	33.59
medium	26.79
bold	25.05
extra bold	24.61
ultra bold	23.01
extra bold cond	28.03
ultra bold cond	26.79

Windsor BERTHOLD

light	25.50

COMPUGRAPHIC

light	29.30
light condensed	34.85
elongated	41.25

WT ITEK

regular	38.24

Zapf Book BERTHOLD

light	21.93
light italic	24.33
medium	20.16
medium italic	21.27
demi	20.06
demi italic	20.75
heavy	18.33
heavy italic	19.33

COMPUGRAPHIC

light	26.66
light italic	27.67
medium	23.81
medium italic	24.66
demi	22.26
demi italic	23.31
heavy	21.43
heavy italic	22.08

MERG LINOTYPE

light	25.78
light italic	26.46
medium	25.46
medium italic	25.78
demi	23.94
demi italic	24.83
heavy	23.39
heavy italic	23.66

MONOTYPE

light	25.71
light italic	26.18
medium	25.54
medium italic	25.94
demi	24.05
demi italic	24.99
heavy	23.85
heavy italic	23.95

Zapf Chancery COMPUGRAPHIC

light	34.75
light italic	36.67
medium	34.21
medium italic	36.17
demi	30.79
bold	28.91

Zapf International BERTHOLD

light	22.16
light italic	24.33
medium	21.82
medium italic	23.26
demi	20.55
demi italic	20.75
heavy	18.89
heavy italic	19.33

	COMPUGRAPHIC
light	24.61
light italic	25.64
medium	24.31
medium italic	25.29
demi	22.23
demi italic	21.98
heavy	20.37
heavy italic	20.79

Zentenar Fraktur BERTHOLD

regular	31.13
medium	30.90

ZF ITEK

45 light	25.14
46 light italic	24.98
55 medium	24.36
56 medium italic	25.38
65 bold	21.97
66 bold italic	22.94
75 extra bold	22.33
76 extra bold italic	22.83

Part VI Copyfitting

These copyfitting programs are to be used in conjunction with the typefactors shown on previous pages and a pocket calculator. The programs are divided into three sections each with its own index page as follows:

index to single lines of type   *page 291*
index to bodytext   *page 295*
index to running text   *page 305*

The variables, or parameters, that need to be known to operate each program are indexed from A–K on each index page. If, for example, the user is calculating for a single line of type and wishes to know the measure that the setting will make, then by reference to the appropriate index the procedure is as follows: solid bullets in the table indicate parameters that are known and a question mark indicates the unknown quantity; the measure is indexed as G and by referring down this column in the table the unknown quantity may therefore be found by using program 5; additionally parameters A, C and E (ie typefactor, number of characters and typesize) must be known in order to make the calculation possible.

A sheet for recording alternative calculations has been included on pages 318/319. It is intended that disposable photocopies of this record sheet be made and used in conjunction with the index pages and copyfitting programs.

It should be noted that the programs in this book have been specifically devised for use with the unique typefactors also shown here. The programs cannot reliably be used with any other method of copyfitting or typefactors.

A single line of type

Parameters covered			C = Number of characters				
A = Typefactor*			E = Typesize				
B = ±letter/wordspace			G = Measure				

PARAMETERS

PROGRAM NUMBERS	A	B	C	D	E	F	G	H	I	J	K
1	●		?		●		●				
2	?		●		●		●				
4	●		●		?		●				
5	●		●		●		?				
3	●	?	●		●		●				

PROGRAM **1**

FOR A single line of type

TO FIND The number of characters

KEYSTROKES	PARAMETERS	TEST
AC	typefactor	26.66
×	measure in picas	15
÷	typesize	10
=	calculator display shows the number of characters	40

PROGRAM **2**

FOR A single line of type

TO FIND Typefactor

KEYSTROKES	PARAMETERS	TEST
AC	typesize	9
÷	measure in picas	15
×	number of characters	50
=	calculator display shows the typefactor required for normal letter/word spacing	30

PROGRAM **3**

FOR A single line of type

TO FIND The number of ± units of letter and
wordspace required to make a given
measure

KEYSTROKES	PARAMETERS	TEST
AC	number of characters	46
−	1	1
= ✕	typesize	10
= M+		
C −	typesize	10
÷	typefactor	26.64
✕	number of characters	46
= +	measure in picas	15
= ✕	12	12
✕	number of units to the em	18
÷ MR		
=	calculator display shows the number of ± letterspace units	−1

PROGRAM **4**

FOR A single line of type

TO FIND Typesize

KEYSTROKES	PARAMETERS	TEST
AC	measure in picas	15
÷	character count	50
×	typefactor	30
=	calculator display shows the typesize in points	9

PROGRAM **5**

FOR A single line of type

TO FIND Measure in picas

KEYSTROKES	PARAMETERS	TEST
AC	typesize	9
÷	typefactor	30
×	character count	50
=	calculator display shows the measure in picas	15

Bodytext

Parameters covered
A = Typefactor*
C = Number of characters
D = Typewritten lines

E = Typesize
F = Interline spacing
G = Measure
H = Column depth

Solid setting programs to find

PARAMETERS

PROGRAM NUMBERS	A	B	C	D	E	F	G	H	I	J	K
7	●		?	●	●		●	●			
8	?		●	●	●		●	●			
10	●		●	?	●		●	●			
12	●		●	●	?		●	●			
13	●		●	●	●		●	?			
16	●		●	●	●		?	●			

With interline spacing, programs to find

PARAMETERS

PROGRAM NUMBERS	A	B	C	D	E	F	G	H	I	J	K
6	●		?	●	●	●	●	●			
9	●		●	?	●	●	●	●			
11	?		●	●	●	●	●	●			
14	●		●	●	●	?	●	●			
15	●		●	●	●	●	?	●			
17	●		●	●	●	●	●	?			

*Typefactor = The number from Part V relating to chosen typeface – or as separately calculated *see pages 226–7*

FOR Bodytext (with interline spacing)

TO FIND The number of characters

KEYSTROKES	PARAMETERS	TEST
AC	typesize	9
+	interline spacing	3
= M+ C	typefactor	26.64
×	measure in picas	15
×	column depth in picas	62
×	12	12
÷	typesize	9
÷ MR =	calculator display shows the number of characters	2 753

PROGRAM **7**
FOR Bodytext (set solid)
TO FIND The number of characters

KEYSTROKES	PARAMETERS	TEST
AC	typefactor	26.64
×	measure in picas	15
÷	typesize	9
×	column depth in lines of type	62
=	calculator display shows the number of characters	2 753

PROGRAM **8**
FOR Bodytext (set solid)
TO FIND Typefactor

KEYSTROKES	PARAMETERS	TEST
AC	typesize	9
÷	measure in picas	15
÷	column depth in lines of type	62
×	character count	2 753
=	calculator display shows the typefactor for normal letter and word spacing	26.64

FOR Bodytext (with interline spacing)
TO FIND The number of typewritten lines
required to convert into an area of set
text with given parameters

KEYSTROKES	PARAMETERS	TEST
AC	typesize	9
+	interline spacing	3
= ×	typesize	9
×	average typewritten line length in picas	24
= M+		
C	typefactor	26.64
×	measure in picas	15
×	column depth in picas	62
×	6 (for elite typewriter) or 7.2 (for pica typewriter)	6
÷ MR		
=	calculator display shows the number of typewritten lines required	57

PROGRAM **10**

FOR Bodytext (set solid)

TO FIND The number of typewritten lines required to convert into an area of set text with given parameters

KEYSTROKES	PARAMETERS	TEST
AC	typefactor	26.64
÷	typesize	9
×	measure in picas	15
÷	average typewritten line length in picas	24
×	column depth in lines of type	62
÷	2 (for elite typewriter) or 1.66 (for pica typewriter)	2
=	calculator display shows the number of typewritten lines required	57

FOR Bodytext (with interline spacing)

TO FIND Typefactor

KEYSTROKES	PARAMETERS	TEST
AC	typesize	9
+	interline spacing	3
= ×	typesize	9
÷	measure in picas	15
÷	column depth in picas	62
×	character count	2 753
÷	12	12
=	calculator display shows the typefactor for normal letter and word spacing	26.64

PROGRAM **12**

FOR Bodytext (set solid)

TO FIND Typesize

KEYSTROKES	PARAMETERS	TEST
AC	typefactor	26.64
×	measure in picas	15
×	column depth in picas	62
÷	character count	2 753
×	12	12
= √	calculator display shows the maximum typesize set solid	10.4

PROGRAM **13**

FOR Bodytext (set solid)

TO FIND Column depth in lines of type

KEYSTROKES	PARAMETERS	TEST
AC	typesize	9
÷	typefactor	26.64
÷	measure in picas	15
×	character count	2 753
=	calculator display shows the column depth in lines of type	62

FOR Bodytext (with interline spacing)

TO FIND Interline spacing

KEYSTROKES	PARAMETERS	TEST
AC	typefactor	26.64
÷	typesize	9
×	measure in picas	15
×	column depth in picas	62
÷	character count	2 753
×	12	12
= −	typesize	9
=	calculator display shows the required interline spacing in points	3

PROGRAM **15**

FOR Bodytext (with interline spacing)

TO FIND Measure in picas

KEYSTROKES	PARAMETERS	TEST
AC	typesize	9
+	interline spacing	3
= ×	typesize	9
÷	column depth in picas	62
÷	typefactor	26.64
×	character count	2 753
÷	12	12
=	calculator display shows the measure in picas	15

PROGRAM **16**

FOR Bodytext (set solid)

TO FIND Measure in picas

KEYSTROKES	PARAMETERS	TEST
AC	typesize	9
÷	typefactor	26.64
÷	column depth in lines of type	62
×	character count	2 753
=	calculator display shows the measure in picas	15

PROGRAM **17**

FOR Bodytext (with interline spacing)

TO FIND Column depth in picas

KEYSTROKES	PARAMETERS	TEST
AC	typesize	9
+	interline spacing	3
= ×	typesize	9
÷	typefactor	26.64
÷	measure in picas	15
×	character count	2 753
÷	12	12
=	calculator display shows the column depth in picas	62

Running text

Parameters covered
A = Typefactor*
C = Number of words/characters
E = Typesize
F = Interline spacing
G = Measure
H = Column depth
I = Pages for visual material
J = Number of prelim/postlim pages
K = Extent of book in pages

Solid setting programs to find

PARAMETERS

PROGRAM NUMBERS	A	B	C	D	E	F	G	H	I	J	K
19		?	●		●	●	●	●	●	●	●
20		●	?		●	●	●	●	●	●	●
23		●	●		?	●	●	●	●	●	●
25		●	●		●	?	●	●	●	●	●
26		●	●		●	●	?	●	●	●	●
29		●	●		●	●	●	●	●	●	?

With interline spacing, programs to find

PARAMETERS

PROGRAM NUMBERS	A	B	C	D	E	F	G	H	I	J	K
18		?	●		●	●	●	●	●	●	●
21		●			●	?	●	●	●	●	●
22		●			●	●	?	●	●	●	●
24		●			●	●	●	?	●	●	●
27		●			●	●	●	●	?	●	●
28		●			●	●	●	●	●	●	?

*Typefactor = The number from Part V relating to chosen typeface – or as separately calculated see pages 226–7

FOR Running text (with interline spacing)

TO FIND The number of words

KEYSTROKES	PARAMETERS	TEST
AC	typesize	10
+	interline spacing	3
= ×	typesize	10
= M+		
C −	number of chapters in book	20
= ÷	3	3
−	number of prelim/postlim pages	10
−	number of pages given over to visual material	34
+	total extent of book in pages	54
= ×	typefactor	26.64
×	measure in picas	15
×	column depth in picas	25
×	2	2
÷ MR =	calculator display shows the number of words	512

PROGRAM **19**

FOR Running text (set solid)
TO FIND The number of words

KEYSTROKES	PARAMETERS	TEST
AC	typesize	10
×	6	6
− M+		
C −	number of chapters in book	20
÷	3	3
= −	number of prelim/postlim pages	10
−	number of pages given over to visual material	34
+	total extent of book in pages	54
= ×	typefactor	26.64
×	measure in picas	15
×	column depth in lines of type	23
÷ MR =	calculator display shows the number of words	511

PROGRAM **20**

    FOR Running text (set solid)

    TO FIND Typesize

KEYSTROKES	PARAMETERS	TEST
AC −	number of chapters	20
÷	3	3
= −	number of prelim/postlim pages	10
−	number of pages given over to visual material	34
+	total extent of book in pages	54
= ×	typefactor	26.64
×	measure in picas	15
×	column depth in picas	25
÷	character count	3 000
×	12	12
= √	calculator display shows the maximum typesize set solid	11.5

FOR Running text (with interline spacing)
TO FIND Interline spacing

KEYSTROKES	PARAMETERS	TEST
AC —	number of chapters	20
÷	3	3
= —	number of prelim/postlim pages	10
—	number of pages given over to visual material	34
+	total extent of book in pages	54
= ×	typefactor	26.64
÷	typesize	10
×	measure in picas	15
×	column depth in picas	25
÷	character count	3 000
×	12	12
= —	typesize	10
=	calculator display shows required interline spacing in points	3.3

FOR Running text (with interline spacing)
TO FIND Measure in picas

KEYSTROKES	PARAMETERS	TEST
AC −	number of chapters	20
÷	3	3
= −	number of prelim/postlim pages	10
−	number of pages given over to visual material	34
+	total extent of book in pages	54
= M+ C	typesize	10
+	interline spacing	3
= ×	typesize	10
÷	typefactor	26.64
÷	column depth in picas	25
×	character count	3 000
÷	12	12
÷ MR =	calculator display shows the measure in picas	15

FOR Running text (set solid)

TO FIND Measure in picas

KEYSTROKES	PARAMETERS	TEST
AC —	number of chapters	20
÷	3	3
= —	number of prelim/postlim pages	10
—	number of pages given over to visual material	34
+	total extent of book in pages	54
= M+ C	typesize	10
÷	typefactor	26.64
÷	column depth in lines of type	23
×	character count	3 000
÷ MR =	calculator display shows the measure in picas	15

FOR Running text (with interline spacing)
TO FIND Column depth in picas

KEYSTROKES	PARAMETERS	TEST
AC −	number of chapters	20
÷	3	3
= −	number of prelim/postlim pages	10
−	number of pages given over to visual material	34
+	total extent of book in pages	54
= M+ C	typesize	10
+	interline spacing	3
= ×	typesize	10
÷	typefactor	26.64
÷	measure in picas	15
×	character count	3 000
÷	12	12
÷ MR =	calculator display shows the column depth in picas	24.4

FOR Running text (set solid)

TO FIND Column depth in lines of type

KEYSTROKES	PARAMETERS	TEST
AC −	number of chapters	20
÷	3	3
= −	number of prelim/postlim pages	10
−	number of pages given over to visual material	34
+	total extent of book in pages	54
= M+ C	typesize	10
÷	typefactor	26.64
÷	measure in picas	15
×	character count	3 000
÷ MR =	calculator display shows the column depth in lines of type	22.5

FOR Running text (set solid)

TO FIND Number of pages available for visual material

KEYSTROKES	PARAMETERS	TEST
AC	typesize	10
÷	typefactor	26.64
÷	measure in picas	15
÷	column depth in lines of type	23
×	character count	3 000
= M+		
C −	number of chapters in book	20
÷	3	3
= −	number of prelim/postlim pages	10
+	total extent of book in pages	54
= −		
MR =	calculator display shows number of pages available for visual material	34

FOR Running text (with interline spacing)

TO FIND Number of pages available for visual material

KEYSTROKES	PARAMETERS	TEST
AC	typesize	10
+	interline spacing	3
= ×	typesize	10
÷	typefactor	26.64
÷	measure in picas	15
÷	column depth in picas	25
×	character count	3 000
÷	12	12
= M+		
C −	number of chapters in book	20
÷	3	3
= −	number of prelim/postlim pages	10
+	total extent of book in pages	54
= −		
MR =	calculator display shows number of pages available for visual material	34

FOR Running text (with interline spacing)
TO FIND Total extent of book in pages

KEYSTROKES	PARAMETERS	TEST
AC	number of chapters in book	20
÷	3	3
= +	number of prelim/postlim pages	10
+	number of pages given over to visual material	34
= M+ C	typesize	10
+	interline spacing	3
= ×	typesize	10
÷	typefactor	26.64
÷	measure in picas	15
÷	column depth in picas	24
×	character count	3 000
÷	12	12
= +		
MR =	calculator display shows the total extent of book in pages	54

FOR Running text (set solid)
TO FIND Total extent of book in pages

KEYSTROKES	PARAMETERS	TEST
AC	number of chapters in book	20
÷	3	3
= +	number of prelim/postlim pages	10
+	number of pages given over to visual material	34
= M+		
C	typesize	10
÷	typefactor	26.64
÷	measure in picas	15
÷	column depth in lines of type	23
×	character count	3 000
= +		
MR =	calculator display shows the total extent of book in pages	54

Record Sheet

Program No	**A** Typeface	**B** ± units letter-spacing	**C** No of characters	**D** No of type-written lines of copy	**E** Typesize

F Interline spacing	**G** Measure	**H** Column depth	**I** No of pages for visual material	**J** No of prelim/ postlim pages	**K** Total extent of book in pages

Bibliography

British Standards Institution
BS 5261: Copy Preparation and Proof Correction, Parts 1 and 2
BSI, London, 1975

Butcher, J
Copy-Editing
Cambridge University Press, 1975

Craig J
*Designing with Type:
A Basic Course in Typography*
Pitman, London, 1980

*Phototypesetting:
A Design Manual*
Pitman, London, 1978

Crouwal W
Proposal for a New Alphabet
de Jong & Co, Hilversum, 1967

Garland K
Graphics Glossary
Barrie & Jenkins, London, 1980

Gates D
Type
Pitman, London, 1973

Haley A
Phototypography
Robert Hale, London, 1981

Hart H
*Rules for Compositors
and Readers*
Oxford University Press, 1967

Hostettler R
The Printers Terms
St Gallen, Switzerland, 1949
Redman, London, 1959

Hurlburt A
Layout: the Design of the Printed Page
Watson-Guptill, New York, 1977

Jacob H
Publishung Terms
Macdonald and Jane's,
London, 1976

Jaspert W, Berry W, Johnson A
Encyclopedia of Type Faces
Blandford, London, 1970

King JC, Esposito T
The Designer's Guide to Text Type
Van Nostrand Reinhold,
New York, 1980

Plumb D
Design and Print Production Workbook
Workbook, 1978, 7 Springfield Road, Teddington, Middlesex, TW11 9AP

Rosen B
Type and Typography
Van Nostrand Reinhold,
New York, 1976

Ruegs R, Froch G
Basic Typography
Academy Editions, London, 1972

Spencer H
The Visible Word
Lund Humphries, London, 1969

Pioneers of Modern Typography
Lund Humphries, London, 1969

Sutton J, Bartram A
An Atlas of Typeforms
Lund Humphries, London

SEE **aliassing** page 22